"Paul Hinlicky d
story of Lutheran
ous generation.
theologians, and controversies in the history of ...
theology, he also provides us with a sound launching pad for new developments. His masterful combination of breadth with nuance and insight makes his *Lutheran Theology* an essential guide for understanding this conflicted but generative theological tradition."

**—Lois Malcolm**, Luther Seminary


"Few could author such an authoritative, searching, and engaging account of the development of Lutheran theology as Paul Hinlicky has done in this concise Cascade Companion. As dense with learning as it is alive with provocation, Hinlicky's fine study tells the tale of Lutheran theology in such a way that no faithful reader will be able to fall back into reductive and overly simple views of what it has meant across the centuries—and so yet means—to think theologically as a Lutheran."

**—Philip G. Ziegler**, University of Aberdeen


"Reading this important introduction to the foundations and evolutions of the Lutheran theological tradition will put any reader in an excellent place to do the faithful creative work in theology that Hinlicky rightly asserts needs to be done today."

**—Jennifer Hockenbery Dragseth**, Mount Mary University

"Paul Hinlicky's book on *Lutheran Theology* through its main epochs is thought-provoking and sharp. He avoids many possible pitfalls focusing on both innovation and corruption in the Lutheran theological tradition. Regardless of one's own position, the clear force of this book is its emphasis of the ambiguities in the Lutheran tradition, and the insistence that these ambiguities are intimately related to the cornerstone, that God alone is the true problem of humankind. Thereby, reminding the reader that even larger problems emerge if one ignores it."

**—Bo Kristian Holm**, Aarhus University, Denmark

# LUTHERAN THEOLOGY

# CASCADE COMPANIONS

The Christian theological tradition provides an embarrassment of riches: from Scripture to modern scholarship, we are blessed with a vast and complex theological inheritance. And yet this feast of traditional riches is too frequently inaccessible to the general reader.

The Cascade Companions series addresses the challenge by publishing books that combine academic rigor with broad appeal and readability. They aim to introduce nonspecialist readers to that vital storehouse of authors, documents, themes, histories, arguments, and movements that comprise this heritage with brief yet compelling volumes.

RECENT TITLES IN THIS SERIES:

*Angels, Worms, and Bogeys* by Michelle A. Clifton-Soderstrom
*Christianity and Politics* by C. C. Pecknold
*A Way to Scholasticism* by Peter S. Dillard
*Theological Theodicy* by Daniel Castelo
*Basil of Caesarea* by Andrew Radde-Galwitz
*A Guide to St. Symeon the New Theologian* by Hannah Hunt
*Reading John* by Christopher W. Skinner
*Forgiveness* by Anthony Bash
*Jacob Arminius* by Rustin Brian
*The Rule of Faith: A Guide* by Everett Ferguson
*Richard Hooker: A Companion to His Life and Work* by W. Bradford Littlejohn
*Scripture's Knowing: A Companion to Biblical Epistemology* by Dru Johnson
*John Calvin* by Donald McKim
*Rudolf Bultmann: A Companion to His Theology* by David Congdon
*The U.S. Immigration Crisis: Toward an Ethics of Place*
    by Miguel A. De La Torre
*Theologia Crucis: A Companion to the Theology of the Cross*
    by Robert Cady Saler
*Theology and Science Fiction* by James F. McGrath
*Virtue: An Introduction to Theory and Practice* by Olli-Pekka Vainio
*Reading Kierkegaard I: Fear and Trembling* by Paul Martens
*Deuteronomy: Law and Covenant* by Jack R. Lundbom
*The Becoming of God: Process Theology, Philosophy, and Multireligious Engagement* by Roland Faber

# LUTHERAN THEOLOGY

*A Critical Introduction*

PAUL R. HINLICKY

CASCADE *Books* • Eugene, Oregon

LUTHERAN THEOLOGY
A Critical Introduction

Copyright © 2020 Paul R. Hinlicky. All rights reserved. Except for brief quotations in critical publications or reviews, no part of this book may be reproduced in any manner without prior written permission from the publisher. Write: Permissions, Wipf and Stock Publishers, 199 W. 8th Ave., Suite 3, Eugene, OR 97401.

Cascade Books
An Imprint of Wipf and Stock Publishers
199 W. 8th Ave., Suite 3
Eugene, OR 97401

www.wipfandstock.com

PAPERBACK ISBN: 978-1-4982-3409-2
HARDCOVER ISBN: 978-1-4982-3411-5
EBOOK ISBN: 978-1-4982-3410-8

## Cataloguing-in-Publication data:

Names: Hinlicky, Paul R., author.

Title: Lutheran theology : a critical introduction / by Paul R. Hinlicky.

Description: Eugene, OR: Cascade Books, 2019. | Cascade Companions. | Includes bibliographical references and index.

Identifiers: ISBN 978-1-4982-3409-2 (paperback). | ISBN 978-1-4982-3411-5 (hardcover). | ISBN 978-1-4982-3410-8 (ebook).

Subjects: LCSH: Theology—Doctrinal—Lutheran. | Luther, Martin, 1483–1546.

Classification: BX8065.3 H57 2020 (print). | BX8065.3 (ebook).

Scripture quotations are from the New Revised Standard Version Bible, copyright © 1989 National Council of the Churches of Christ in the United States of America. Used by permission. All rights reserved worldwide.

Manufactured in the U.S.A.                    05/04/20

To the Institute of Lutheran Theology:
Independent, Rigorous, Committed

# CONTENTS

*Preface* • ix

Introduction: A Conflicted Tradition • 1

1 The Theology of the Cross as Program of Reform • 13

2 From Confessionalism to Orthodoxy • 34

3 The Idealistic Theology of Liberal Lutheranism • 87

4 Neo-Orthodoxy and the Renewal of Trinitarianism • 106

Conclusion: A Brief Prolegomena to Any Future Lutheran Theology • 166

*Bibliography* • 171
*Index of Names* • 181

# PREFACE

When I originally conceived of this book I had planned a concluding chapter surveying the contemporary scene in Lutheran theology. Surely the purpose of an introduction, if we are beginners, is to bring us to the present task of an intellectual tradition that we would see continue into the future. Or, if we are outsiders, we want to acquire sufficient orientation to interact knowledgeably with representatives of this tradition, whether from the past or in the present. In either case, the work of writing an introduction to a theological tradition is itself a work in contemporary theology! In other words the book here presented contains implicitly and in many places explicitly commentary on the contemporary scene in Lutheran theology.

Truth be told, after five hundred years Christian theology in Luther's tradition may have reached a point of dissipation and exhaustion on the one side or the sterility of mere repetition of erstwhile certitudes on the other. Whether and how it continues forward, both faithful and creative, rests upon what readers of an introduction like this will do with the knowledge acquired. A story of Lutheran theology from its origins up to the preceding generation will unfold in what follows, which can serve as a launching pad for new endeavors in the present for the future.

Since any number of possible, if not mutually compatible future trajectories exist for Lutheran theology, it is more useful to offer a critical introduction unveiling how the distinct and even contradictory epochs of Lutheran theology can and did, each in its own way, find a specific resource in Luther. The premise of the story to be told is that a perpetually recurring appeal to represent the "genuine" Lutheran theology is an idle, if not basely self-justifying gesture—a grim irony upon a theological tradition that primordially denies the possibility of self-justification! The responsibility is thus laid instead upon a reader who would take up the tradition of Christian theology initiated by Luther in the present for the future. This introduction succeeds to the extent that it equips and requires intellectual honesty in one's act of appropriation of this particular tradition of theology.

For appropriation, especially of an iconic figure like Luther, always and necessarily does some violence with respect to the original intentions of founding figures, embedded as those are in an historical horizon that has passed irretrievably away. In any case, as important as the volcanic personality of Luther was and remains for Lutheran theology, it is a misleading oversimplification to make him founding hero, or for that matter, villain in one's theology. Do not say, "This is Luther—end of discussion!" That is a kind of fundamentalism: "Luther said it. I believe it. That settles it!" But rather say, "Here is my Luther—for whom, begging your pardon and his, I am responsible." In the latter

*Preface*

case one makes oneself open and vulnerable to critique one's own act of appropriation. Critique, in turn, depends objectively on whether one's reading of Luther is a good one that does justice to all the evidence, especially evidence that cuts against the grain of one's own appropriation. A bad reading, however, is just the gross or sophisticated dishonesty of selective proof-texting from a supposedly sacrosanct authority who in fact remains profoundly controversial—even, if not especially when he is understood well.

While I have sought in what follows to avoid stridency and treat partisans fairly, the author's present stance will be visible in many places, but especially in his continuing resistance to the linguistic policing by contemporary theological revisionism with respect to the ecumenical tradition of biblical language about God. I have long agreed with Robert Jenson that God's self-identification with the Crucified frees us from the need to find God by the projection of our own qualities upon a blank screen. I worry with Karl Barth that today's revisionists wittingly or not fall into the Feuerbach trap in their enthusiasm for a "relevant" and "constructive" theology. Construction in any case is not "creation out of nothing," but interpretation, if it intends orthodoxy, of the ecumenical tradition's biblical language about God—which is just what early Lutheran theology claimed over against recent "innovations." And relevance like beauty is in the eyes of the beholder.

I am happy here to acknowledge, however, a little gesture signifying hope for the future of this tradition coming from theologian Sarah Hinlicky Wilson, who is also my daughter. She has lived courageously as a theologian in her own right during troubling times when the nominally Lutheran denominations in the USA hardly support rigorous theology in Luther's tradition any longer, while the self-consciously secular academy has still not overcome its allergy

*Preface*

to Christian theology in any iteration. In the recent past, she challenged this technological Neanderthal who is your present author to join her in a theological podcast, *Queen of the Sciences.com*, which—in spite of the tongue-in-cheek title—has already acquired a worldwide audience thanks to Sarah's globetrotting ministry within the ecclesiastical family of the Lutheran World Federation. She also did me the honor (once again) of reading a draft of this book, supplying valuable comments and corrections. At the end of her notes on the draft, she wrote the following words which can serve as a segue to the introduction of this book and supply at least a glimpse of what that missing final chapter on the contemporary scene would indicate.

> I would suggest you specify right at the outset that not only is this a history of Lutheran theology, not Luther's, but also that it is a specific intellectual trajectory within Lutheran theology, namely, one that is primarily concerned with (1) justification by faith, (2) the distinction between law and gospel, and (3) the credibility of both Jesus and the Scripture as the 'word of God' when faced with particular historical and intellectual challenges. Then I would suggest you openly acknowledge the strands of Lutheran theology that you are therefore *not* covering. For example: the history of missionary thought, beginning with Bartholomäus Ziegenbalg's initiating and sympathetic study of Indian religion, up to and including African theologians like Gudina Tumsa arguing for the 'objects' of mission to be recognized as 'subjects' and 'agents' of their own evangelization; or the theological contributions of women, who for entirely obvious reasons were generally not awarded a space in the

> intellectual tradition and yet intervened in the ways available to them, from Argula von Grumbach's challenge to the Ingolstadt theologians, to Catharina Regina von Greiffenberg's wildly popular doctrinal poetry on the incarnation of Christ, to the many women in Scandinavia who wrote hymns, like Birgitte Boye and Lina Sandell, or played leading roles in the development of diaconia, like Mathilda Wrede and Elisabeth Fedde. I suggest, further, it would be politic to observe with joy the entry of many women into the intellectual conversation in recent decades!

To which this author replies with delight, "Well roared, young lioness!" As explained in the Introduction, my selection of themes and focus for this book is defined by the strict rendering of theology as disciplined "knowledge of God." Much is overlooked by this narrow focus, as Sarah rightly notes, since the knowledge of the God meeting human need is a variegated tale and the specificity of "Lutheran" theology consists in the saving God rescuing the helpless sinner. Hopefully what is accomplished by this strict and narrow focus—what makes any theology theological is its claim to knowledge of God—aids and abets us in the tasks to which she rightly summons the present generation for the sake of the future.

Finally a note on sources. I have limited notations to the essential direct references and resisted the scholarly temptation to fill out obsessively the endnotes with the provision of additional warrants, proof texts, secondary sources and learned digressions. I have freely drawn on and adapted any number of my previously published works, which contain more technical discussions and ample documentation of the matters covered in this book.

*Preface*

Where I thought it helpful, I have referred the reader in the endnotes to those places for further study. The bibliography contains not only the works cited but also works that the author recommends for further study.

PAUL R. HINLICKY

Time after Pentecost, 2019

Introduction

# A CONFLICTED TRADITION

IN 2017 LUTHERAN THEOLOGY observed the momentous occasion of its five-hundredth anniversary. Observances of this milestone, however, wavered between slick presentist celebrations hyping Luther as the origin of all that is good about modernity,[1] many sober commemorations in ecumenically sensitive academic or ecclesiastical events, and even lament—as in Michael Massing's massively researched but invidious comparison of a proto-Trumpian "evangelical" Luther over against a proto-"progressive" Erasmus.[2] This manifestly divergent range of evaluations reflected the decidedly mixed blessing of a decidedly

---

1. The documentary by Rick Steves, *Luther and the Reformation*, *2017*, was widely distributed in the Evangelical Lutheran Church in America.

2. Massing, *Fatal Discord*.

conflicted legacy with its own origin in a controversy that has still not been mastered.

In fact, even naming this tradition of Christian theological reflection "Lutheran" is controversial—going back to Luther himself who protested against using his name! Yet it is the literary legacy of Martin Luther that of necessity provides an objective baseline for the following study of "Lutheran" theology. In his own lifetime Luther authorized publication of his collected writings and provided introductions to guide future readers. Thus our procedure in referencing Luther texts in this study is well grounded historically, provided that we do not take even these late-in-life constructions of his writings by Luther himself uncritically. For it was from the colored perspective of many-sided conflict that Luther warned about misreading his earlier writings. Upon critical examination, the discerning reader of this book will be able to discover in Luther's introductions to his writings reasons for the perennially conflicted state of "Lutheran" theology—in the central matter no less of his signature doctrine of justification![3]

More broadly, any intellectual tradition with a centuries-long history will inevitably betray multiple intersecting but also diverging streams, subsurface currents, eddies, and whirlpools—or, to change the metaphor into Deleuzian terms, rhizomatic outgrowths and lines of flight when its original inspiration is captivated and retooled by alien projects. The further from the source the "Lutheran" tradition of theology flows, it experiences clarification and enrichment

---

3. "Preface to the Wittenberg Edition of Luther's German Writings, 1539," *Luther's Works* [hereafter LW] 34:279–88; and "Preface to the Complete Edition of Luther's Latin Writings, 1545," LW 34:323–38. Twentieth-century Lutheran research went on a wild goose chase in search of Luther's so-called "tower experience" as the "Reformation breakthrough" in which Luther came to the totally forensic conception of righteousness extrinsically attributed to the believer.

## A Conflicted Tradition

and/or contamination and confusion and/or both, as the case may be. An introduction is thus needed to navigate a maze which cannot be defined but only broadly described as "Lutheran theology."

Early Lutherans conceived of their theological work as a return to the ancient Christian tradition of theology which had been in recent centuries corrupted—so they claimed—by "papist" innovations. This was to be a return to the "clear and pure fountain of Israel," thus locating their own theological work in the tradition of the gospel as descended from the Scriptures of Israel and, as Luther once put it, their "proclamation" by the New Testament. In view of this complexity of a tradition which consciously locates itself within a broader tradition as a renewal of the latter, an "introduction" of necessity simplifies. It simplifies not only by presenting a drastically reduced selection of themes for consideration according to what is deemed essential in the author's judgment, but also in ranking these chosen themes and relating them to one another in an historical narrative. Inevitably such selections and rankings and connections reflect an author's contemporary concerns. But even more simplistic are the usual introductions which would identify some timeless essence of the subject matter and lay it out in pristine purity. This procedure aspires to a full objectivity in so far as it conceals the theological subjectivity of its author and the author's contemporary audience. This introduction by contrast takes an alternative route of tracing the Lutheran theological tradition through its major epochs showing how both innovation and corruption could resource itself in the textual legacy of Martin Luther.

In addition to the general problem of navigating the complexities of continuity and discontinuity in an intellectual tradition, then, we have a specifically Lutheran complication: from the beginning, Lutheran theology has been an internally conflicted tradition, such that what counts as "authentically" Lutheran has itself often been a matter of intense dispute among self-identified "Lutherans." It is undoubtedly the case that other Christian intellectual traditions witness the same internal tensions, since traditions are in any event not monolithic blocks but agreed-upon arguments, often so ferocious that the common question framing disputes becomes obscured in the fog and friction of battle. In any case, what constitutes an intellectual tradition is more agreed-upon questions for inquiry rather than any set of pat answers. What are the questions to which the famous slogan of the Lutheran Reformation—Christ alone by faith alone, by grace alone, by the Scriptures alone—is the answer?

Historical-critical knowledge of the original framework of inquiry to which this confession of faith and critical reflection on it in theology was addressed as known from Luther's texts establishes a certain baseline by which to judge consequent appropriations. It is the case, however, that subtle transformations in the framework of inquiry have occurred throughout the Lutheran theological tradition. Is Lutheran theology to be conceived of as a revolutionary break from the medieval past of Christendom—repudiation of academic (= "scholastic") theology in favor of pure biblicism? Or is it to be thought of as a reform movement within the church Catholic? Is it to be regarded as pioneering the path forward to the egalitarian modern world by way of the European Enlightenment and the rise of science? Or, on the contrary, do its conservative tendencies and political quietism perpetually incubate fascist reaction? Is it to be regarded as the fecund progenitor of many-headed and market-responsive Protestantism or a degenerate lunge into sectarianisms inevitably devolving into present post-Christian neo-paganism?

## A Conflicted Tradition

Theological traditions, to be sure, produce doctrine or dogma (Christine Helmer[4]) and one might consider the classical doctrines of early Lutheranism as the matter to be explored in an introduction. True, but this production of doctrine, even at its origin, is an historical process of critical appropriation from an ecumenical heritage and its critical projection into a unknown future. A theologically critical introduction, then, educates its readers into this ongoing process of reflection and engagement.

The big picture of these five hundred years may be sketched as follows. First, there are the formative years of Martin Luther's creative public work as a reforming theologian within the Western Catholic Church. This was followed, second, by the rise of Lutheran confessionalism amid rival confessionalisms from the 1530 Augsburg Confession onward through the German Lutheran consolidation in the 1580 Book of Concord,[5] which formed the theological basis for the epoch of confessional Lutheran Orthodoxy that followed in the seventeenth and into the eighteenth century. At the beginning of the age of Enlightenment, Lutheran Orthodoxy began to unravel under the combined impact of the rise of the natural sciences, which theology experienced internally in the rise of biblical criticism. But rationalistic Lutheran Orthodoxy was also undermined by the emergence of the Pietist movement, which subverted orthodoxy's virtually exclusive ecclesiological emphasis on purity of doctrine, exposing to view born-again Christians in other than the purely Lutheran church. As we shall see, however, both of these subsequent developments of Orthodoxy and Pietism could appeal to the historical Luther. His free criticisms of biblical books were appropriated by the

4. Helmer, *End of Doctrine*.

5. Kolb and Wengert, eds., *Book of Concord*, all citations will be taken from this edition.

new biblical critics while his Augustinian theology of the affections was reclaimed by the Pietists.

In the nineteenth century a new form of Lutheran theology emerged from these upheavals under the name of "liberalism." Liberal theology continued impulses from both biblical criticism and Pietism, but developed them in terms of a scheme of progressive revelation, culminating in the supreme idea of God as love as manifest in the perfect God-consciousness of the human Jesus. Since the great Enlightenment philosopher Immanuel Kant had ruled out of rational bounds any theological claim to know God, liberal theology undertook inquiry into what remained: historical knowledge of human representations of God which it then organized in an evolutionary scheme of progressive historical development. A minority theological reaction against liberalism during the this epic could be described as "neo-confessionalism" which in vain tried to disrupt the liberal scheme of an immanent and progressive evolution of divine representations in human history by asserting the "paradox" of an absolute revelation in time and space, as may be seen above all in the lonely witness in the 1840s of the Dane Søren Kierkegaard.

The twentieth century witnessed would-be revivals of all these previous types of Lutheran theology: there was a notable "Luther Renaissance" circling around the publication of Luther's massive literary output known as the Weimar Edition. Lutheran confessionalism revived especially in Germany and in the United States, often derisively named "Neo-Orthodoxy," albeit in a decidedly conflicted relationship with the pioneering Swiss Reformed theologian, Karl Barth, who in any case hardly deserves the derision and may rather, as we shall see, be described as a crypto-Lutheran! In contrast to neo-confessionalism, attempts were made to revive seventeenth-century Orthodoxy especially in North

America, while a school of thought gravitating towards liturgical renewal and fresh ecumenical engagement emerged under the banner of "evangelical catholicism."

Repristinating forms of Orthodox Lutheran theology inevitably assume the continuing viability of Aristotelian natural philosophy and metaphysics in which this type of Lutheran theology was enmeshed, along with scholastic methods of deductive argumentation from first principles supposedly supplied in the supernatural revelation of an inerrant Bible. This would-be revival of Lutheran Orthodoxy stands in sharp distinction from twentieth-century neo-confessionalism, which privileged the theology of the young Luther, including his decisive break from Aristotelianism. Twentieth-century neo-confessionalism, in a covert acknowledgment of the collapse of the "great chain of being" under the impact of Darwinian biology, allied itself with emergent existentialist philosophy drawing upon the aforementioned Kierkegaard. But this alliance with existentialism seemed unholy to critics like Karl Barth who regarded it as yet another philosophical captivity and loss of theological freedom.

The foregoing big picture serves to indicate how challenging it is to reduce Lutheran theology to a manageable topic narrowly defined—in any case an "essentialism" that is to be rejected methodologically. And yet this historical course of Lutheran theology over the centuries may be seen to have been prefigured embryonically in the course of Luther's own theological career, as the textual evidence of his literary legacy indicates. As all the later developments of Lutheran theology can in fact claim to have a basis in the creative but also polemical episodes of Luther's life-work, such prefiguring of Lutheran theologies in Luther himself should not be surprising even if it becomes visible only in hindsight. It can in any case service heuristically, providing a series of significant theological themes stemming from Luther and permitting us to observe as milestones the diverse ways in which these themes were appropriated by later proponents of Lutheran theology in response to new and different historical challenges.

We will label the formative and creative period of Luther's own reformatory theologizing after his early neologism, the "theology of the cross." This designation indicates a sharply critical perspective on hitherto predominant forms of theologizing, which he rejected in turn as "theology of glory." It is this critically awakened perspective on the folly and stumbling block to be affirmed theologically in proclaiming "Christ crucified," which, as we shall see, generates the familiar but still much misunderstood Reformation doctrine of justification by faith alone. It is this key affirmation of "faith alone," moreover, that requires hermeneutically the proper distinction within God's word between law and gospel, judgment and pardon, demand and promise, reward (or penalty) and gift. This proper distinction is necessary for the sake of the holy and lifegiving use of the Scriptures. This proper employment of Scripture as parsed by the proper distinction between God's law and God's gospel succeeds in proclamation of the real and saving presence of the embodied Christ, as Luther's reforming theology came to full expression in the test case concerning the Lord's Supper. The reformatory Luther's theology of the cross thus culminates in its own peculiar theology of glory as Luther affirmed christologically that it is the glory of our God to come down to the depths and into human hands to eat and drink.

In Luther's own lifetime, however, his theologizing turned from the cruciform mode of protest to a mode of construction, assuming responsibility for the renewal of European Christendom in the territories that had received his reformatory theology. Luther approved of his colleague Melanchthon's Augsburg Confession as a positive statement of faith according to which churches would be reformed and henceforth organized. Against the skeptical Erasmus Luther dogmatized: "take away assertions and you take away Christianity!" So already in Luther the positive formulation of Christian teaching took the form of public confession, "doctrine" or "dogma." Theology now became church dogmatics after the models of Luther's catechisms on one side and Melanchthon's "topical" method (*loci communes*) on the other. Yet, as the Reformation protest simultaneously fractured into multiple forms of Protestantism, and as Roman Catholicism likewise emerged from the fray as a still dominant yet all the same competing form of Christianity among rival others, confessionalism became polemical, orthodox, and dogmatic, charged with the task of delimiting its own one and only true church from competing rivals.

As mentioned, the most significant internal divergence from Luther in this development in the epoch of Orthodoxy was the rehabilitation of Aristotle to serve as a platform for dogmatic argument and construction. Thus Luther's theological method of arguing for the truth of the gospel by means of scriptural exegesis had to be reconceived as a foundationalist claim for the miraculous status of the Bible—the doctrine of verbally inerrant inspiration, which is still the official axiom of fundamentalist versions of Lutheranism. Luther's assertion of Scripture as the literary source of the gospel's claim to truth was thus converted into an Aristotelian claim for the Bible as the axiomatic, for divinely given, first principle. The Latin instrumental ablative, *sola scriptura*, "by the Scriptures alone," was taken as a nominative, "only the Bible"—a highly convoluted stance since it presupposed Aristotle's organization of rational inquiry in order to assert "only the Bible" as an axiom from which deductions could be drawn and processed into mandatory articles of belief,[6] including such essential matters as an historical Jonah being swallowed by a some kind of whale.

In time, this exaggerated claim for the Bible as a treasure chest of revealed propositions demanding assent had to lead in turn to exaggerated criticism of the Bible to show that it could not bear this epistemological burden. As the rise of the natural sciences and its empirical method undermined especially the plausibility of the deductive argumentation in Aristotle's biology, cosmology, and metaphysics, the form of Lutheran theology in orthodoxy that had wedded itself to Aristotle likewise tumbled and fell like the fabled walls of ancient Jericho. The emerging biblical critics circled the citadel of scholastic Lutheranism as "the true visible church of God on earth:" they blew their horns at the Jericho wall of the divinely dictated and inerrant Scripture which had been erected as a mighty fortress in counterpoint to the infallible dictations of a divinely instituted papacy. Thus both Protestant and papist idols fell in the eyes of enlightened Europeans. Truth be told, however, Luther could also be claimed as a source not only in undermining the authoritarian papacy but also in undermining the authoritarian biblicism, since he had rather freely practiced historical criticism himself, having learned the method from the Renaissance humanist Lorenzo Valla's exposé as a forgery of the Donation of Constantine (alleging the first Christian emperor's gift of political authority in the West to the Bishop of Rome). Luther's nascent historical criticism was there for everyone to see in his various introductions to newly translated books of the Bible.

Picking up the pieces after biblical criticism, liberals like Albrecht Ritschl retooled Luther's distinction between

---

6. See Lutheran Church Missouri Synod, "Statement of Scriptural and Confessional Principles."

## A Conflicted Tradition

God hidden and God revealed for a theology of progressive revelation according to which the Spirit-guided historical evolution of the picture and/or concept of God left behind primitive, wrathful, vengeful depictions of God in paganism and Judaism in order to reach its pinnacle in Luther's idea of God as love (even though admittedly some remnants of "Catholic superstition" remained in Luther). In this way, according to liberal theology, Luther actually re-established for church and theology the simple, authentic faith of the Jesus of history in God as a kindly heavenly parent.

Our introduction to Lutheran theology will proceed accordingly. In chapter 1 we will inspect the core reformatory theological proposals given rise by Luther's theology of the cross in the doctrines of justification by faith, the distinction of law and gospel, and the real presence of Christ in the Lord's Supper. In chapter 2 we will investigate the positive articulation of these theological themes in the dogmatic theology of classical Lutheranism in its pitched battles with Calvinism, Catholicism, Radical Reformation "enthusiasm," and emergent freethinking in the context of disputation over "the true visible church of God on earth." In chapter 3 we will understand how biblical criticism arose at least in part as a legitimate development of the Lutheran tradition's "epistemology of access," which distinguishes between the gospel word of God spoken in the resurrection of the crucified Jesus and addressed to all nations and the many words of God recorded in the Scriptures. Likewise in chapter 3 we will note how Pietism's theology of the heart recalled neglected aspects of Luther's teaching on justifying faith in the period of Orthodoxy. In chapter 4 we will survey the significant Lutheran representative in liberal theology, Albrecht Ritschl, under the marching order, stemming from the philosopher Immanuel Kant, to erect "the Kingdom of ends" on the earth. In our final chapter 5 on the Neo-orthodox Lutheran theology of the twentieth century, we will point to some of the more creative attempts to continue but also to resolve the conflicted tradition of Lutheran theology by re-grounding it in the classical doctrine of the Trinity, albeit confusedly at times by appearing to be a revival of the idealism of the post-Kantian philosopher, George Friedrich Hegel.

# 1

# THE THEOLOGY OF THE CROSS AS PROGRAM OF REFORM

THE CONTROVERSY OVER THE sale of indulgences that broke out after Luther posted his famous Ninety-Five Theses in October 1517 proved to be little more than an opening skirmish. It surprised many observing the five-hundredth anniversary of this event recently to learn that the theologian-monk who instigated this skirmish was actually defending a certain view of "purgatory." The first of his theses read, "when our Lord and Master Jesus Christ said, 'do penance,' he meant for the entire life of the Christian to be one of repentance." In other words, purgatory is not to be deferred to some future state after death but begins here and now with baptism. The purging of sin begins already now in the new Christian life of daily and lifelong repentance.

In making this argument, Luther took sides with the view that purgatory denoted deliverance from sin, not punishment for sin. It was this latter view of purgatory as punishment, on the other hand, which stood behind the lucrative traffic in indulgences, to which the Augustinian friar pastorally objected. The objection was twofold: if outstanding punishment required by retributive justice could be satisfied with an ecclesiastically sanctioned ransom payment, the penitent is cheated of genuine repentance and thus deliverance from the grip of sin upon heart and mind and body. In the Ninety-Five Theses that punitive scheme was reduced to absurdity with the second objection. Luther wrote hypothetically that if purgatory was divine punishment for sin, and if the pope truly had rightful authority to satisfy such punishment by granting indulgences from the treasury of the surplus merits of Christ and the saints, why wouldn't the pope out of Christian love just give a free pass to any and all suffering in painful purgatory? Opponents had a difficult time responding and the argument quickly moved beyond the initial dispute over the marketing of papal indulgences to the authority of the pope as such.

By April of the following year, Luther had had time to reflect upon the deeper issues involved in the controversy regarding authority in theology and issued several sets of theses for debate within his order of Augustinian Friars. The *Disputation against Scholastic Theology*[1] argued that a root assumption about human powers was being made in medieval academic theology—in Luther's time already nearly a four-hundred-year-old institution!—namely, that human beings by virtue of their existing powers can at least will to will the love of God. The correlate of this

1. Luther, *Disputation against Scholastic Theology*, LW 31:3–16.

## The Theology of the Cross as Program of Reform

optimistic natural anthropology was an equally optimistic natural theology: surely the good and merciful Perfect Being would in turn be obligated by its own perfection to reciprocate this minimal natural effort of his own creatures. Luther's root argument is chiefly directed against theologians nearer in time to him like Gabriel Biel, William Occam, and Duns Scotus (proponents of the "modern way" as it was called), while Thomas Aquinas (standard-bearer of the "ancient way" in scholastic theology) was faulted chiefly for having introduced Aristotle's assessment of natural human powers as a kind of philosophical baseline for Christian theological anthropology. Luther, by the way, knew the material well: he had been lecturing on Aristotle's ethics in particular for a number of years.

Luther has two objections to this root assumption regarding natural human powers. First, essentially the creature is obligated to the Creator, not the Creator to the creature. Second, recalling the church father Augustine and especially his anti-Pelagian writings, which Luther had recently discovered and studied intensely, human creatures existentially, in their existing condition of fallenness, are unable even to will the love of God, rigorously considered. This becomes clear, particularly when the unique and supreme love owed to the Creator of all that is not God is taken as the Scripture's First Commandment. One might perhaps want to love God above all but mere desire or intention is not the resolute act of will required, when God is taken seriously as God beside whom there is no other. What is revealed by this reflection is rather the impotence of human will and its captivation by a deep, obsessive, and all-pervading self-concern: "concupiscence," or the "lust for domination," in Augustine's language. Thus, as Luther put it, fallen "man wants to be God and does not want God to be God."

What we discover here in Luther's critique of scholastic theology is a retrieval, which Luther expressly acknowledges in a number of places, of the fifth-century church father Augustine's profound insight into human bondage as a social or corporate condition of sinfulness, as this had previously been figured by Paul the apostle in the first ancestor, Adam. For Augustine all the Christian knowledge of God is represented by this Pauline juxtaposition of existential ways of being in relation to God, whether in Adam or in Christ. Of course a definite paradox attends this Pauline-Augustinian insight and its retrieval by Luther. If one is in fact in bondage to sin and thus captive to flattering self-deception on account of it, how can anyone come to stand out of this situation of captivation sufficiently even to see the chains that in reality bind? So the question of epistemic access arises and becomes acute.

In a second set of theses, the *Heidelberg Disputation*,[2] Luther provided a revolutionary resolution of this conundrum which he now specified, following the Apostle Paul: access to genuine knowledge of God and self-knowledge comes about by the disruption of the existing self at the intervention of the christological paradox of the cross through the folly of preaching. In 1 Corinthians 1, Paul discusses the paradox or stumbling block which is inalienably presented in the Christian message of the "gospel" of a "crucified Christ." Luther interprets this to mean that the Christian message comes as news of an event that pertains to the self yet cannot otherwise be known or accessed: it comes to the existing self from outside of itself in order to transform. The very form of this message is likewise external to the existing self: it is the preaching or proclamation of an event.

This is "folly" because it is not wisdom that is naturally available; theology is not Socrates's midwifery of the

2. Luther, *Heidelberg Disputation*, LW 31:35–70.

## The Theology of the Cross as Program of Reform

soul. Access to God's saving event must rather be created by a disruptive intervention. This external word of proclamation offends against any optimistic notion that human beings should be able on the basis of their existing selves and natural powers to seek and find God, even if in reality as creatures they are naturally obligated to do so. Instead of that, the folly-form of preaching, announcing an historical event of saving and transformative significance, executes a fundamental reversal: it is God who seeks and finds, just as those who are sought and found are perforce robbed of the illusion that by their own reason or strength they can rise up to God for safety, healing, or wholeness. Furthermore, the paradoxical form of preaching reflects and reinforces the unheard-of content of the proclamation, which Paul names "Christ crucified—a folly to Greeks and a stumbling block to Jews."

Why is that? The term Christ means Victor, like Joshua conquering Canaan or David seizing Jerusalem. When Messiah comes he comes as Victor, just as the Palm Sunday crowds greeted Jesus's entrance into Jerusalem, "Hosanna to the son of David!" So if the content of Paul's proclamation of good news from God is "Christ crucified" that is like saying "Victor victimized," "Joshua put to the sword," or "David defeated by Goliath."

One can take a contradiction in terms like this in one of two ways. Either it is taken as pure nonsense or it is taken as a striking rhetorical form that wants to communicate something for which there is no existing vocabulary-cum-concept—just because it refers to a new reality intervening in and disrupting the familiar world. The latter is Luther's meaning in his "paradoxical" theology of the cross. The new reality, hitherto unknown, which Luther discovers in his theology of the cross is *agape* (the Greek word in the New Testament for divine and creative love): "the love of the cross, born of the cross, which does not seek a good to enjoy but confers a good upon a bad or needy person." So Luther concluded the *Heidelberg Disputation* with its innovative interpretation of the knowledge of God.

Luther undertook this program to reform theology for the sake of a clear and salutary enunciation of this event of creative divine love actualized in the proclamation of Christ crucified on behalf of the weak and the ungodly. Its critical power was to oppose any and all the ambiguous and often toxic efforts of religious people to merit a favorable status with the divine by their own upward spiritual mobility. The theology of the cross executes a prophetic judgment, not merely on the obvious wickedness of barbaric and profane people but especially on the devious wickedness of civil and religious people. Self-justification is exposed as the devious sin of good people. Faith by contrast will be recommended as the surprising righteousness of trusting in one's justification as the merciful deed and gift of God.

This sin of faithless self-justification is not only seen in the contemptuous attitudes of superiority typical of "insiders" over against "outsiders," such as in Jesus's parable of the Publican and the Pharisee. Luther sees sublime sin in humanity's allegedly highest virtue: the naturally elicited love of God which he had attacked in the *Disputation concerning Scholastic Theology*. In Luther's caustic analysis, however, this merely natural law amounts only to the religious climber's realization that piety pays; a healthy dose of spirituality is in one's enlightened self-interest. So he names this naturally elicited love of God "concupiscent" love, that is, selfish, greedy love that loves God not for God's sake but for one's own. One loves God poisonously when love seeks for itself to gain reward and avoid pain—as codified in the usual theologies of heaven, hell, and purgatory. Luther formulates his theology of the cross to target exactly such

## The Theology of the Cross as Program of Reform

greedy love of God, because in its self-deception it confuses everything, calling good evil and evil good.

But the good of the cross, surprisingly, is that it spiritually crucifies the naturally selfish lover of God; apart from this death of the sublime sinner, the creative divine agape love cannot actually find the "bad and needy person," hidden behind the gleam and glitter of religious works, upon which to lavish its divine new-creative flood of agape love. Note well: Luther's polemic is not directed against "good" works but the "religious works" invented by spiritual seekers to placate or impress the deity. What is at issue, then, is what makes truly good works good. Luther's answer will be christologically shaped: a truly good work comes about when the Christian believer loves the neighbor in the world just as Christ has come into the world and made a neighbor of the believer.

This insistence on the needed transformation of the existing self, and the harshly provocative language Luther employs to accentuate it, undoubtedly constitutes the most difficult challenge to contemporary understanding of Luther's theology of the cross. It can sound perverse, as if the more one hates oneself, the more lovable one becomes to God. Perhaps that danger of some kind of new cross-mysticism is why Luther eventually abandoned the rhetoric, if not the substance, of his early theology of the cross. Many current social-liberationist theologies construe the theology of the cross in an exclusively horizontal fashion, however, leaving out of the picture what is of central concern for Luther: the real God who for true human good crucifies the existing self spiritually by laying the cross of Christ upon it. Luther's focus on the transformation to theological subjectivity cannot thus but be lost from view. Correspondingly, it has become common today even when invoking Luther's precedent in the theology of the cross, to reduce the crucifixion of Jesus either to the dastardly human act of Roman imperialism crushing a Jewish patriot or as the human act of exclusivist Judaism in cahoots with Rome against the subversively inclusive Jesus. There may be important aspects of truth in these purely horizontal interpretations of the theology of the cross, but they miss what is crucial for Luther and his reform-theology, namely, that apart from divine and radical surgery by way of the believer's own "Gethsemane of the soul" in spiritually laying the cross of Christ upon the existing self, God's love for the ungodly cannot reach us in the profound self-deception of sublime self-seeking.

A brief excursus in the form of a cautionary tale is appropriate here: the pro-Nazi, so-called "German Christians" of the 1930s similarly rejected Luther's accent in the theology of the cross on the spiritual crucifixion of the self-seeking self. These Nazi sympathizers called for a "positive Christianity" with worship that would be a good-feeling "celebration" of the existing self of the Aryan nation in place of worship that would summon forth the struggling new creation of God to engage in lifelong repentance. German Christianity accordingly invoked the "heroic" spirit of Luther, meaning his iconic willingness to stand up to Pope and Emperor. Yet this was a heroism sans Luther's "conscience bound to the Word of God" as famously confessed at the Diet of Worms. The abortive "Bethel Confession" of 1933, co-authored by Dietrich Bonhoeffer and Herman Sasse (which we will discuss in some detail in chapter 4), put its finger on the root of the problem with the pro-Nazi German Christians. It again and again invoked Luther and his legacy to reject enthusiastic adulation of Adolf Hitler as a new savior sent from God on the grounds that the Holy Spirit is not given apart from the external word concerning

## The Theology of the Cross as Program of Reform

Christ crucified. What is "spiritual," then, is not seeking but rather being found.

By the early 1520s, Luther had come to his mature doctrine of justification by faith alone, although, as we shall shortly see, it was not without ambiguities that would haunt the future of Lutheran theology. Perhaps the essential text in this regard is Luther's treatise *On the Freedom of the Christian*.[3] It begins with the Pauline paradox (see Galatians 5:12–13) that the Christian is a perfectly free "lord" subject to none and yet, at the same time, this same Christian is a perfectly dutiful servant subject to all. The meaning of the paradox is that the Christian is liberated, set free, to love. In this way Luther mirrored the argument of Paul in Galatians, where the apostle rejected imposition of circumcision on Gentile converts: "For freedom Christ has set you free. Therefore do not submit again to the yoke of bondage." But only, Paul continues, let not your freedom become license for the greedy self-serving behavior of the old self. Instead "in love become slaves to one another." Following Paul in this way, the old canard that Luther abolishes "good works" is thus manifestly false. In dispute, as previously mentioned, is rather what is the "good" in "good works."

For Luther good works are categorically not "religious works" by which the existing self seeks security or blessing, whether to avoid the pains of hell or to gain the rewards of heaven. Truly good work is revealed in the life-culminating-in-death on the cross of Jesus Christ who became a slave to set others free. The good works of the Christian are and only can be participation in this one good work of Jesus Christ. Following Paul once again, Luther names this participation "faith": "it is no longer I who live but Christ who lives in me; and the life I now live in the flesh I live by the faith of the Son of God who loved me and gave himself

3. Luther, *On the Freedom of the Christian*, LW 31:327–78.

for me." Thus when Luther added the adverb "alone" (a corresponding Greek word is not there in Paul's original language) to his translation of Romans 3, "we hold that a human being is justified by faith *alone*," the point was not to exclude the new life of the believer transformed by faith with its repentance, but rather to specify this new life with its "good" work as life in Christ. Like its parallels "by grace alone," or "by Scripture alone," Luther's "by faith alone" serves to clarify what is primary in such a way as to exclude all rivals, namely, Christ alone as the doer of the good in whom believers participate by faith operative in love.

And that specification is the point of the correlative doctrine of the "proper" distinction between God's law and God's gospel. The point is to make unmistakably clear that only Christ delivers from the holy predicament of divine and holy judgment upon the self-deceived servant of sin. It is important here not to take the term, "law," as denoting something like "ethics" in our contemporary usage: ethically, there is no difference between law and gospel. Both have as their content the instruction to love of God above all and love of one's neighbor as one self—as both self and other creatures are in and under the creative love of God. It is crucially important not to take the term "law" philosophically as "ethics" or juridically as civic rules but theologically as denoting God coming in the office of judge. What is involved is the knowledge of God in his history with creatures. In Luther's reform theology, the term "law" does not denote either ethics or legislation but is used strictly theologically to bespeak the God who judges. The cognate term, "justification," whether it be by works or by faith, in any case refers to how the human being stands before the God of the prophets who searches and judges the heart.

Thus the proper distinction between law and gospel arises directly out of the theology of the cross and its

## The Theology of the Cross as Program of Reform

identification of Christ alone as the sinner's righteousness, thus leading directly to the doctrine of justification by faith alone in Christ alone. Already in the Heidelberg Disputation Luther made the crucial argument that the most salutary doctrine of God's law cannot and does not help the indicted sinner find justification. Rather, its holy function is the opposite of such help; its function in the hands of the Holy Spirit is to reveal the impotence of the existing self in its self-seeking bondage to sin so that God can breakthrough to perform his proper work of the divine and creative agape love, justifying the ungodly.

"Improper" distinctions between law and gospel, in this light, are many. For example, commonplace is the distinction between Judaism and Christianity, or between shadow and substance, or between Old and New Testaments, or between human legalism and divine permissiveness, or between rote ritual and existentially genuine personal conviction, or between rigid dogma and creative freethinking and so on. Another kind of misunderstanding of the distinction occurs when it is turned into a hermeneutical Procrustean bed into which all the various genres of Scripture must be forced. For example, one might ask whether divine commands like, "Let there be light," or "Come, follow me" are to be classified as law or gospel. Are beatitudes like, "Blessed are the hungry for they shall be filled," law or gospel? In fact Scripture contains many genres and rhetorical forms. It also contains not only the talk of God but various discourses about God. None of the interpretive problems involved here, which necessarily precipitated, as we shall see, the rise of biblical criticism later on in the history of Lutheran theology, are resolved by Luther's proper distinction of law and gospel, which has rather to do with the prophetic preaching of God coming in judgment and the apostolic preaching of the reconciling God who in the person of his crucified Son meets this very divine judgment on behalf of those thus prophetically indicted in God's controversy with his wayward creation.

In the course of this treatise *On the Freedom of the Christian*, Luther makes several discrete arguments for justification by faith aside from the exegetical one from Paul that we have just reviewed. One argument is that faith is justice or righteousness because it gives God what is God's due, namely, all the glory for all his rich mercy in Christ to those undeserving of it. In this explanation, the essence of justice is to give to each his or her due, which is precisely what the sinner's faith does in glorifying God for his grace. Another argument is that faith is the bridal pledge of the soul in response to the bridegroom-Christ's nuptial vow, "I am yours and you are mine." In this case faith is that which honors the justice or righteousness of Christ in his remarkable gift of himself in a "joyful exchange" with those who otherwise would not or could not be righteous. In either case faith justifies because it glorifies the God of grace concretely by giving to Christ one's sin to bear away and in its place making one's own Christ's righteousness freely offered.

Interpreters have sometimes shied away from these ancillary arguments for justification by faith because they seem to indicate that Luther sees in the justified sinner a real if inchoate righteousness. The fear is that that implication of human transformation would undermine the external nature of the righteousness that is Christ's alone as the agent who accomplished it and in strict logic is as such credited or attributed to the believer as a gift, who in her own reality is and remains a sinner. From this valid concern arose the "forensic" doctrine of justification which is the metaphor of God the judge pronouncing a verdict of not guilty upon the guilty sinner. But the concomitant subordination or even rejection of the motif of the joyful

## The Theology of the Cross as Program of Reform

exchange comes at the severe cost of truncating the christological backbone of Luther's theology of justification and in turn obscuring Luther's account of the transformation of the existing self in the gift of faith—which is for Luther the new birth from above by the Spirit and the actual good reason to speak of "justifying faith."

To be sure, when the justice of the justified sinner consists in the justice of giving God glory for undeserved mercy, it is impossible for that justified sinner ever to rely before God on its own achieved progress in faith or holiness. Analyzed more abstractly, this account of justification by faith insists that the paradoxical righteousness of the justified sinner remains extrinsic to the existing self and consists entirely in the unmerited grace of God communicated to it in the event of preaching Christ crucified for us, be it by sermon or by sacrament. This explanatory interpretation of justification by faith identifies the Christian life as a "passive life," continually created by the ever new communication of the unmerited grace of God. The real righteousness is God's alone, who is essentially God who gives, ever generous, ever gracious. In this sense the righteousness of grace remains "alien" to the believer as Creator is ontologically other than creature. Existentially sinners justified by faith remain through all the twists and turns of life ever dependent on fresh enunciation of the life-giving Word of God.

As mentioned, this account is named "forensic" justification, reflecting the metaphor of the courtroom where the divine judge pronounces the guilty one nevertheless to be innocent in a sheer fiat. The sheer fiat would be acceptable if we had in mind by it the creative command of God in Genesis 1: "let there be . . ." The divine declaration performs in this linguistic action creative agape love. It makes what it speaks. If employed in an exclusive and one-sided way, and denuded

25

of the Creator's creativity in speaking, however, forensic justification's declaration of the sinner's righteousness as an act of sovereign grace can hardly avoid the suspicion that we have to do here with a "legal fiction," in which God privileges the impenitent with favor if only they do the one good deed of believing that they are not intrinsically righteous. And so we are back to the danger in the rhetoric of the theology of the cross, that the more sinful one regards oneself, the more status one acquires with God.

Sensing this danger, Luther quite deliberately sustained the supplementation of the forensic interpretation of justification by faith with the equally biblical metaphor of the marriage of Christ with the believing soul—often abbreviated to "union with Christ." Indeed Luther's rich views of the vital roles that Christ and the Spirit respectively play in justification arguably become far more visible in this account, which might be called "effective" justification, since in this account the transformation of the existing self into the new person of faith by Spirit-wrought union with Christ cannot be overlooked. It is rather the engine that powers the machine.

As Luther imagines it, what happens in preaching or sacrament is not a sheer announcement of abstract grace, but a mediated communication of concrete grace. The crucified and risen Christ is in person this concrete mediator who is really present in word and sacrament. He comes as a suitor wishing nuptials. He says to the sinful soul, "Give me your sins and take my righteousness. Give me your death and take my life. Give me your poverty and take my riches." This communication aims at a transaction, an exchange, just as premodern marriage was also a new economic relationship. Translating the Latin of the church fathers, *commercium admirabile*, into the German, *fröhliche Wechsel*, Luther called this a "joyous exchange": joyous just because

## The Theology of the Cross as Program of Reform

it is not the usual tit-for-tat quid pro quo of the marketplace in which one gets (at best) what one is owed. Rather this is an unheard-of, astonishing exchange in which the present Christ comes to give all things, but especially himself in his once-for-all life and death for others, and in the process takes all upon himself that otherwise weighs down the intended recipient to eternal death. In the Spirit-wrought obedience of faith, a new self emerges in this joyful transaction just as in a true marital union man and a woman become husband and wife. Bold and living faith arises by the work of the Spirit, which takes to heart Christ in his nuptial promise as one's very own.

Here we come to Luther's famous accent on the "promeity" (Latin: *pro me* = "for me") of justifying faith. To be sure, for Luther the existing self cannot talk itself into faith or otherwise maneuver to the conviction from one's heart that Christ has lived, died, and now reigns for me. In the joyful exchange, Christ not only takes on the believer's doubt but gives in its place his own Spirit to bestow faith's fullness of conviction, namely, that "I am Christ's and Christ is mine." Thus Luther's transformation of the believer is and remains at the mercy of the Spirit. The Spirit is needed for the daily conviction of faith in the sense of belonging to Christ because of Christ amid trial and testing and in spite of the persistence of sin. To be sure, if ever this account of effective justification by faith is taken in a one-sided way, the crucial role played by the Holy Spirit in generating and sustaining faith can disappear. Faith then inevitably comes to be regarded as an act of human willpower. Thereby a tremendous burden falls upon the anxious believer to maintain her relationship to Christ and in this foolish way to deserve what can never be deserved—the unmerited grace of God. But note well—the problem in this unhappy development, as we shall see when we discuss Lutheran Pietism in the next chapter, does not come by supplementing forensic justification with effective justification—which is precisely how Luther argued in the seminal treatise *Freedom of the Christian*—but rather it comes by an under-appreciation for the vital yet distinct roles of Christ and the Spirit in justification by faith.

We have seen how in the perspective of the theology of the cross Luther's reformatory doctrine of justification by faith alone arises and with it the proper distinction between law and gospel for the scriptural preaching of God's Word, specifically the good news of the resurrection of the crucified Jesus and what that means for captivated sinners. What Luther took for granted in his early theology, however, was a certain corresponding view of Christ's person and work contained in the motif of the joyful exchange which was (and remains) in tension with other views of Christ prevalent in the Western Latin Christian tradition. Luther's view of Christ was a laser beam focused on the unity or singularity of the person of Christ. For Luther the great Christ-hymn of Philippians 2 narrates the historical journey of a single subject. In view is the journey from an antecedent condition of equality with God to a self-giving act of humility in relation to God in becoming human and obedient in his assumed human flesh, even to death on the cross, and thence the one-and-the-same person's exaltation to reign as Lord in equal esteem with God over a redeemed creation. The single person of Christ thus passes through states of humiliation and exaltation; crucially, it is as this exalted one who had once been humiliated that the one Christ now is and can be really present in his word and sacrament to speak ever new to human auditors his nuptial promise. Thus Christ can be heard by them with repentance and faith where and when the Spirit of the exalted Christ grants access.

## The Theology of the Cross as Program of Reform

But the traditional ecclesiastical terminology regarding "natures" divine and human can mislead us by subsuming creative divinity and created humanity under a common concept, "nature." Luther's view of the incarnation certainly appropriates the teaching of the church fathers from the Council of Chalcedon on the "two natures," in order to say that in the single phenomenon in the world which is Jesus Christ crucified and risen we encounter at once and inseparably creative divinity and created humanity. The danger in the traditional concept, however, is that we regard divine and human natures as some kind of static blocks of underlying substance—a conceptual separation that militates against the saving perception of the unity of Christ's person. But in theology this philosophical terminology of "nature" serves merely as a conceptual placeholder for the eminently biblical distinction of Creator and creature.

For Luther the point of the two-natures doctrine in Christology is precisely not forever to separate Creator and creature into incompatible metaphysical entities—a consistently Platonic thinking that led the ancient arch-heretic Arius astray, as the opponent of Arius, Athanasius detected. Rather the gospel point of the two-natures doctrine was to indicate the dynamic and saving movement of the Creator to embrace the lost and fallen creature so that this embraced creature may freely and joyfully turn from sin and return thanksgiving and praise to the Creator. The person of the divine Son becomes incarnate in an action that consists in the singular, personal communication of divine and human properties in the one Christ to accomplish the mission of redemption. In this light, Luther organized his view of deviant teachings that undermine the gospel around this christological axis: some, he said, deny the divinity of Christ, others deny his humanity, and yet others deny the saving work which the singular God-man accomplished for lost and hapless humanity.

It is not then as though, for Luther, that a divine nature is one sort of substance and human nature is another sort of substance and somehow these substances collaborate in Christ as if personal agents. Such a virtually Nestorian Christology of the two sons, one of Mary and one of God, was frequently how the incarnation was interpreted in the Latin West in so far as it came to treat "natures" philosophically as quasi-agents rather than theologically as conceptual placeholders. Going all the way back to the Tome of Pope Leo, one might say that it is the divine nature that forgives sins and heals the sick but it is the human nature that grows weary and hungry and finally dies on the cross. For Luther, however, this is to treat "natures" as real things or personal agents rather than as conceptual baskets describing the characteristic possibilities of things or persons—in this theological connection, the possibilities of the Creator of all that is not God on the one hand and of the creatures that Creator God creates on the other hand. It is the one person of the Son of God with his assumed humanity who is the sole agent and subject of christological doctrine, employing divine and human possibilities according to the exigencies of his saving mission.

When we treat "natures" in Luther's way with the view to their mutual communication of created and creative possibilities in the person of the incarnate Son on his mission of redemption, we lift up the free act and obedience of the divine person described in Philippians 2; by the same token this free act of intra-divine obedience of Son to Father is not only made intelligible but seen as necessary teaching for us to understand Christ in his promised salvation of captivated humanity. This human individual, this fellow creature in our midst, Jesus, does divine things; he forgives sins, heals the sick, raises the dead, and stills the storm. This divine Son of God, equal to the eternal Father in divine majesty and glory, freely out of love undertakes and suffers human things; he grows weary and faint, suffers thirst and dies in the profoundest condition of dereliction. In this way of a reciprocal communication of properties divine and human, the one Jesus Christ the Son of God passes through a state of humiliation to the glory of his exaltation to the end of the redemption of the lost creation.

Luther articulated this Christology, which he had actually presupposed from the beginning inasmuch as it is the backbone of his teaching on the "joyful exchange," in two great treatises from later in the 1520s: *This is My Body*[4] and *Confession concerning Christ's Supper*.[5] Because the reality of Christ's presence in his exalted body became controversial with other concurrent attempts at reformation, which later consolidated into the Reformed and Anabaptist confessions, Luther's Christology has often been treated as an ad hoc rationalization for his still half-way papist views on the Lord's Supper. Such a reading is manifestly erroneous.

No one more vehemently denied that the Lord's Supper was an ecclesiastical work by which the clergy could still the anger of God at the sins of the laity by a "sacrifice" of the transubstantiated body. The idea here was that the clergy had the power to confect the body and blood of Christ in the Eucharist and offer it back to the offended God on behalf of sinful people. Proto-Protestants like Karlstadt and Zwingli could only view Luther's affirmation of Christ's bodily presence in the Lord's Supper as a still-papist rationalization that lent value to the mass as a sacrificial offering. They did not see that Luther's affirmation of Christ's bodily presence was in fact cut from the same

4. Luther, *This is My Body*, LW 37:3–149.
5. Luther, *Confession concerning Christ's Supper*, LW 37:151–372.

cloth as his rejection of the medieval theory of transubstantiation, dependent as that also was upon Aristotelian categories of substance and accident, to provide a theoretical explanation of the real or bodily presence of Christ promised in the institution of the Lord's Supper.

Luther reasoned here by analogy: as the divine person is to the human body-and-soul in the incarnation so the risen Christ is to the loaf singled out in the sacramental action of the Lord's Supper by the performance of Christ's word of promise, "This is my body given for you." Just as the human body-and-soul of Jesus does not cease to be truly human when it is appropriated in the incarnation by the divine person of the Son of God, so the loaf of bread does not cease to be truly bread when it is appropriated by the crucified-and-risen Christ as the vehicle of his promised presence. Given the unity of person, however, Christ's genuine presence can only be as the very body-and-soul, our human brother, that the divine Son once became and forever now remains. And in this case, the point of Christ's real presence in the Lord's Supper is not to lend sufficient value to the priest's offering of the transubstantiated elements to God to appease anger and still divine wrath. Reconciliation of the holy God and sinful humanity has been accomplished once and for all at Golgotha! Indeed, the exalted Christ can be present anywhere—for Luther he may be called upon even from the pit of hell (so Jonah prayed from the belly of the sea monster, according to Luther, and there was heard). Yet he wills and pledges himself to be present in his saving reality "for us" where and when bread and wine are publicly set apart for believers to eat and drink according to his "last will and testament."

Thus far more than an esoteric debate about Christ's presence in the Lord's Supper was at stake in Luther's eucharistic controversies alike with papists and Protestant

## The Theology of the Cross as Program of Reform

alternatives; indeed what is at stake cannot be swept under the rug with a vague appeal to a so-called "real" presence—what other kind of presence is there than a real one? Presence is "being there"—somewhere in time and space. Thus what was at stake in the dispute was the here-and-now "reality" of the one Jesus Christ the Son of God, inclusive always of the human body-and-soul which he became and which he remains for us and our salvation. Just as the theology of the cross gave rise to the doctrine of justification by faith alone and with it the proper (hermeneutical) distinction (not metaphysical dualism) between law and gospel, it necessitated in turn the real, that is to say for us earthlings, the bodily presence of the singular subject of the incarnation, the Son of God who came in the flesh, the divine Logos incarnate. Controversy made it clear to the would-be reformer of Western Catholic Christianity that this dogma or doctrine of Christ as true Savior had to be asserted, warranted, and sustained against fatal deviations which would undermine it. It could not remain merely or silently presupposed.

# 2

# FROM CONFESSIONALISM TO ORTHODOXY

BY THE END OF his life the prodigious Luther had produced voluminous occasional writings—to such an extent that he himself confessed that he could hardly make order or sense out of them all. Many of his writings he had produced burning the midnight oil and in haste rushed off to the printer to address the latest crisis. Some of Luther's most regrettable excesses reflect this posture of a harried, alternately defensive or aggressive polemicist. He rationalized these excesses by falsely maintaining that verbal violence was not actual violence and that in all such matters he left actual violence to the lawful authorities. These writings—demonizing the Pope as the antichrist, fixating upon the devil at work in the rebelliousness of the peasants, judging rabbinic exegesis as demonically blinded and stubbornly resisting the manifest prophecies of Messiah Jesus in the Old Testament text—are cut from the same cloth: Luther's apocalyptic, which frames the Christian gospel in God's macrocosmic conflict with the anti-divine powers of sin, death, and devil. Luther's apocalyptic, however, is both indispensable to understanding his Christian theology and yet also its lethal descent into the human-all-too-human demonization of flesh and blood theological opponents fomenting sinful human violence. Thus in our present post-9/11 world, Luther's biblical theology of the divine warrior emerges as a major challenge going forward to the tradition of Lutheran theology.

The problem involved here is not so simple as the usual "quick fix": the superficial and self-serving Christian contrast between the primitive and vengeful God of the Old Testament and the all good but not quite all-powerful God of the New Testament. Struggle, strife, conflict, trial, and tribulation are at the heart of the canonical biblical narrative of the Testaments; an invidious comparison of a peaceful New Testament with a violent Old Testament is Christian deception and self-deception. Luther confronts us for good or for ill with the inescapable biblical theology of divine violence in that the God of love is zealously, jealously, militantly against what is against love—as twentieth-century Lutheran theologian Paul Tillich once put it. The challenge is how to preserve the virtue of Luther's apocalyptic framing of the macrocosmic conflict of God with the devil while eschewing the vicious business of incarnating the devil as flesh and blood human others, real or imagined. This was a gutter to which Luther too often descended. Or to put the question another way, How is the theopolitics of purity to be trumped by a theopolitics of reconciliation?

If this is the real challenge, however, it is also a mistake, frequently indulged by contemporaries and cut from the same cloth, to demonize Lutheran Orthodoxy (in distinction from critical judgment upon it as also critical appropriation of it such as will be offered in this chapter). Orthodoxy means church preaching, teaching, and practice that run straight and true to the gospel, which in turn ever authors and authorizes the existence and mission of the church. Deviation ("heresy") thus confuses and degrades ("heterodoxy") or even falsifies ("apostasy") the being of the church in Christ in the power of the Spirit. The intention of orthodoxy is thus part and parcel of theology in Luther's tradition.

Critical theology identifies such deviations in order to reject them (the traditional "anathema"). Theology that does not intend orthodoxy is just as much to be faulted, then, as theology that prematurely claims to have achieved orthodoxy. Orthodoxy is teaching in accord with the gospel where teaching is not abstract theorizing but rigorously thinking and articulating all that is logically and materially necessary for the corporate walk of the church in accord with the gospel. In this matter, ever fresh theological work is necessary, as the gospel and the church's life under the gospel in mission to the nations is dynamic; it is perpetually challenged by new and unanticipated circumstances which require innovations ("testing" in the sense of "experimentation"). Orthodoxy, therefore, is the Spirit's work in process. Theology that intends orthodoxy is sine qua non until the consummation judges and resolves all outstanding issues raised by the wayfaring theology of the church militant in time and through space.

The theological task of "testing" (in the sense of judging experiments for fidelity to the gospel) is explicitly mandated in the New Testament: as Mark 13 teaches, testing is needed to distinguish the presence of the authentic Christ who went to the cross for others from pseudo-prophets and pseudo-Messiahs promising escape from trial; as Galatians

6 teaches, it is needed to identify the dawning new creation of the ecclesia of God, keeping it from relapsing back into worldly religiosities, whether of "circumcision or uncircumcision"; as 1 John 4 teaches, testing the spirits is required to see if they acknowledge Jesus Christ as the one who came in the flesh and remains this particular flesh ever after. Note well: the assumption of these texts from across the spectrum of the New Testament is that spirits speak in the world. In the contest of history, the church is at work in a world surfeit with claims to salvation, religious truth, messiahs, and prophets. Even as theology in mission tests in the sense of experimentation, rigorous and continuous testing of the tests is necessary just because some of the needed experiments in theology fail and theology must learn from its own failures.

If we take the era of Lutheran Orthodoxy not as a golden-age once-and-for-all achievement but rather as an historically necessary experiment in the Spirit's work in progress under particular circumstances, the critical question to be raised against it, as we shall see, concerns its loss of the Augsburg Confession's "ecumenical intention"[1] at the hands of a triumphalist ecclesiological claim (made, to be sure, by each and every one of the rival and contending orthodoxies: Roman, Calvinist, Anabaptist, as well as Lutheran), namely, to possess, to the exclusion of others, the true visible church of God on earth. But we are getting ahead of the story.

"Take away assertions and you take away Christianity!" So Luther instructed a foe whom he regarded as brightest and best of all, the fellow humanist, Erasmus of Rotterdam. To label Erasmus in contrast to Luther as a "humanist," as has been common, is to perpetuate a misunderstanding, since Luther too was very much a "humanist"

1. Forell and McCue, eds., *Confessing the One Faith*.

educator. Humanism—the *studia humanitatis*—in the Renaissance was not an ideological position foreshadowing Enlightenment virtues of freethinking and tolerance but an academic and pedagogical method; the "study of humanity" stood for a methodological turn away from the sterility and futility of protological metaphysics, that is, away from the intellectual quest for the origin of things on the supposition that rational ascent to grasp the First Cause would deductively explain in turn all that followed from it in a system of being. It was thus a repudiation of speculation in favor of the down-to-earth "the study of humanity." And since humanity is the animal having language, which is the medium of all human culture, the study of languages with their idioms and rhetoric was paramount in the humanism Luther and Erasmus shared. They both advocated the turn "to the sources" (Latin: *ad fontes*).

So the academic revolution of humanism took place under the supposition that human language, as the pervasive medium, formed the prerequisite of any other possible forms of inquiry including theology, so far as the Bible forms the language of faith. Humanism was the turn from metaphysics to language, particularly in theology to the Hebrew and Greek languages in which the Bible was composed. It was not, however, any kind of rejection of the use of human reasoning by way of rigorous logic. Rather the point was to come to precise and necessary assertions for the sake of the gospel in its mission to the nations in the life of the church. Especially for Luther, then, one should not treat the Bible as a hodgepodge of propositions that theologians get to sort, select, and organize into a system of their own devising according to some metaphysical system. Rather one must read the Bible in a literary way to understand exactly what is being asserted about the saving God and sinful humanity so that Christian theology assists believers in understanding and appropriating, asserting and confessing the truth of the gospel in the present situation. The famous quarrel between Luther and Erasmus was an "in-house" one between fellow "humanists," with Luther accusing Erasmus of getting cold feet at just the moment when their shared reformatory-humanist scholarship was beginning to bear risky fruit for the reform of church and society.

At the end of the treatise against Erasmus, the title of which should be translated "On Captive Choice,"[2] Luther paid Erasmus high tribute. Luther said that Erasmus alone had penetrated to the real issue in the by now wide-ranging dispute over Luther's proposed reformation of Christian doctrine by the newly asserted criterion of justification by faith alone, with its correlates of the proper distinction between law and gospel and the real presence of Christ as saving Lord. Luther's teaching in this treatise pointed to the diagnosis of dire human need behind his doctrinal Reformation: the captivation of human desire by the idols and demons of the fallen creation and its resulting paralysis in relation to God's will.

Reading the Bible in literary fashion, this captivation was seen by Luther as the radical consequence of paradise lost, that is, the loss of true humanity in the broken humanity inherited from the fateful disobedience of the primal father, Adam. What Adam lost in himself and thus for all his descendants was the paradisiacal possibility of a free and true choice for God, for willing the will of God—just as the new Adam, Jesus Christ, will do on behalf of Adam's children once and for all in the Garden of Gethsemane. Henceforth in exile from paradise, all the choices of the children of Adam, even their best civil and religious choices, betray the deeper choice inherited from Adam, namely, to seek self in all things rather than to receive self with all other things as

2. Luther, *Bondage of the Will*.

gift and task from the Creator. Human love or desire, which indeed motivates human creatures in all things, thus also in civil and religious life, has become "curved into itself," as Luther would put it. As such, it can no longer innocently and wholly desire God the Creator and freely and spontaneously do God's will on the earth. If this biblical-narrative diagnosis does not yet convict, Luther finds corroboration in an honest account of human experience, which attests the impotence of the human will to accomplish even the good that it might somehow wish. A will that cannot do that to which it aspires is not free but unfree, impotent.

Luther's opening salvo against Erasmus, asserting the spiritual bondage and impotence of the fallen human will, was foundational in the construction of Lutheran Orthodoxy. It was expressly taken up and affirmed in the 1580 Formula of Concord. Yet the fallacy of equivocation with respect to the crucial terms under consideration, the human free will and its powers, would bedevil the future. It must be borne in mind that "human freedom" or "the freedom of the will" have multiple senses which can confuse the discussion. It is taken to mean freedom of action, that is, the power to do what one wills. But it is also taken to mean the freedom to choose between alternative courses of action. And it can also be taken to mean freedom of desire, doing and choosing voluntarily or willingly. Luther certainly affirms the third sense of freedom; his teaching that faith must be free and joyful, in no way coerced, presupposes such freedom as also his patristic teacher, St. Augustine, maintained. Otherwise one cannot speak of human will at all!

What Luther denied, however, was that desire captivated by idols or enslaved by demons could willingly will the will of God. Captivated desire consequently freely and joyfully sins; all its choices presuppose the sinful, idolatrous self-love bequeathed from Adam. As such human choices are only between the greater and lesser evils of merely civil or political justice. And even if hypothetically one could want to do the will of God, the children of Adam again and again prove themselves impotent to accomplish the will of God. Somewhat incoherently, however, Luther maintained that humans were free with respect to the things "below them." He meant by this the knowledge and capacity to act on the greater and lesser evils of civil or political justice, the various possibilities of economic life and so forth. His rival in reformation, Huldrich Zwingli, drove a truck through that opening Luther created by maintaining freedom over things below humanity! How can God work out the predestination of the saints except through the secondary causes at work in those human things "below them?" Luther's resistance to Zwingli's radical divine determinism, incoherent as it seems, was nevertheless the basis for the Lutheran rejection of the Reformed doctrine of an absolute and eternal decree determining all things down to their finest details, including damnation and salvation.

As pessimistic as Luther's assessment of the now natural powers of the existing self in exile from Eden later seemed in the optimistic eyes of modern culture, it is nevertheless crucial for understanding to see that for Luther the captivation of desire by sin provided the radical leverage by which to criticize prophetically the brutal egoism concealed behind the admirable appearances of civil and religious life. Interestingly, just this leverage is of particular interest today in our current "postmodern" culture which is questioning the modern anthropocene with its titanic construction of a "sovereign self"—the "thinking thing" which controls, manipulates, and predicts all "extended things" as if putty in our hands, molding at will and without limit even humanity's own fragile and ecologically linked human bodies. The twentieth century has taught us what brutality lurks behind this modern posture of "creative destruction," from the dreadful Vietnam logic of "bombing villages to save them" to the upward mobility bromides of the positive-thinking "prosperity gospel" preachers. Disillusioning postmodern culture oscillates dangerously as a result between desperate reaffirmation of sovereign-self utopianism and sober but despairing nihilism. The utopian illusion is all the more stridently affirmed on the one side that we humans are radically free enough and good enough to make all things new, ourselves included. The despairing conclusion on the other side is all the more resisted, that the more things change the more they remain the same, that there is no hope we can believe in. Truth be told, such honest despair lurks just below the surface of our distracted lives. For Luther, however, just this despair of the self in its pretended sovereignty is the Spirit's prosecuting work, preparing the way of God's new creation. God breaks down in order to build up, kills in order to make alive. In other words, only God and God alone is capable of "creative destruction"—and that, not by the sword or the purse, but by his Word and Spirit.

Such are important contemporary considerations for theology in the tradition of Luther. In the now waning era of Enlightenment modernism, Erasmian skepticism is still regarded in some circles desperately holding on to the secular status quo although the thin gruel of its "stillborn God"[3] seems impotent in the face of a Luther who is painted in turn as a ferocious dogmatist—the ancestor of, rather than the antidote to decadent American Christianity, in its faithless quest to secure political patronage.[4] But Erasmus's allegedly modern preference for theological uncertainty betrays upon examination the now tottering dogmatic anti-dogmatism of the secular Enlightenment. Humans will not live by bread

3. Lilla, *Stillborn God*.
4. So I have argued in Hinlicky, *Luther for Evangelicals*.

alone but for good or for ill by every word putatively sounding from the mouth of God.

In this light let us return focus to the more introductory matter: the necessity in Christian theology for claims to truth by way of assertions or predications. It is this for which Luther contended in his treatise against Erasmus's brief for an undogmatic stance of theological agnosticism. Let us try to understand why Luther asserted that "if you take away assertions you take away Christianity" and how this necessity of assertion of truth regarding God and humanity is made for the sake of Christian predication (the Latin word for "preaching" is identical to the word for "predicating": in either case a predicate is assigned to a subject in a statement of human language).

To illustrate: in asserting justification by faith the Christian preacher addresses the sinner as embraced by Christ through the gospel and declares the great Nevertheless that now obtains: "You are now—as joined to the company of Christ the beloved Son by the Spirit—also beloved of God!" This is an assertion, a claim to truth newly connecting God and humanity. Indeed, on analysis this gospel-preaching/predicating consists in a series of such assertions, assertions being statements of what purports to be the case. As we can see in this rudimentary example of gospel preaching-predicating: you are a sinner; Christ embraces sinners; Christ is the beloved Son of God his heavenly Father; a sinner embraced in Christ is therewith also embraced in the Father's love for the Son. If a preacher, however, were to pause and take time to warrant each of these admittedly controversial claims, she would never get around to making the evangelical declaration of the sinner's justification by faith alone in Christ alone—a matter of no little urgency for the preacher of the gospel.

## LUTHERAN THEOLOGY

Our modern objection (though it is as ancient as the complaint of "folly" by the Greek philosophers whom Paul discusses in 1 Corinthians 1) to this matter of urgent Christian predication reflects Erasmus's complaint against Luther: such counterintuitive assertions cannot be held or made with academic certainty; on the contrary, asserting uncertain things is the intellectual vice of fideism (a circular faith in faith) or dogmatism (a self-privileging belief held in defiance of contrary evidence). Indulging such intellectual vices opens up a Pandora's Box of superstition ("enthusiasm") and undermines morality. It is better, argued Erasmus, for Christians to stick with what is existentially certain (just as the ancient Roman skeptic, Cicero, before him and after him the Enlightenment skeptic, Kant, maintained), namely, the Christian's conscientious sense of moral duty. The experience of the moral "ought" in conscience is what is certain. Yet if in place of the clarity of God's gospel-predicating, an alternative clarity is found in the human phenomenon of conscience, manifestly this alternative certainty turns on the presumed power of human free will to know and to do the good, however difficult it may actually be to accomplish what one ought to do rather than succumb to what one is inclined to do. Just this root assumption of Erasmus was the special target of Luther's critique. An impotent will amounts to mere wishing; if it cannot do what it wants, it is not free—just as the Apostle Paul describes in Romans 7.

Theologians in the patient mode of reflection, in distinction from preachers in the urgent mode of assertion, can and do give an account of such basic Christian assertions. They explain what in the world they are talking about. Assertions, if they are to be credible, cannot be pure opinionating. Even to be meaningful, they must refer to something real in the creaturely world of space and time to which others can also refer, no matter how unusually theologians construe such commonly accessible reference points. Centrally for Christian theology is the reference point which is the Jew Jesus crucified under Pontius Pilate. In the light of his resurrection and the believer's resurrection to faith, theologians construe this crucified one as the Lamb of God bearing away the sin of the world. Theologians thus do not warrant Christian assertions in the sense of demonstrating Christian assertions of faith as if to neutral observers. Rather they continually remind believers and unbelievers alike that faith in Christ refers in this world to the crucified One. As such and only as such, they insist, he is and ever remains the object of faith which believes the good news of his resurrection. The task of clarifying what this objectivity means by way of responding to objections and resolving misunderstandings falls to theologians, who hope to achieve the civic peace of humane disagreement with opponents who deny or dispute the baseline Christian predication of "Christ crucified." Luther qua theologian does this work, not least in his energetic arguing against Erasmus's principled agnosticism.

It is not to be overlooked, however, that Luther's Christian-theological assertions have a peculiar and uncanny quality: penultimately, as we just noted, they refer to the crucified Jew Jesus. Just so, however, they refer ultimately and essentially to a heavenly and thus invisible God whose promise of his coming kingdom is not yet publicly fulfilled for all to see and is indeed perceived but dimly by the eyes of faith. Without this reference of Jesus to his heavenly Abba-Father, we would not be referring to the particular Jew who died on Golgotha. The latter-day "radical" Lutheran, Rudolf Bultmann, was right about this: the riddle of the Jesus of history is how the one who proclaimed his heavenly Father came to be the one proclaimed not only by his Easter believers but in the first place by this unseen God in raising him from death. In this respect, the Christian-theological assertions are not based on something for all to see, even believers. It is notable that the New Testament never imagines to describe directly the resurrection of Jesus but only purports to attest its consequences in the empty tomb and the appearances of the risen One. "He is not here—he is risen!" As Bultmann saw, the certainty of faith depends on another sense than seeing; it depends on hearing in the matrix of human language. One cannot see the Abba-Father whom Jesus proclaimed but only hear of him, just as also no one sees the resurrection of the Son by the Father but only hears of it.

This built-in reserve regarding the mysteriousness of gospel talk about God is essential to the theological subjectivity of faith, so that in the world it remains in the vulnerable posture of a "hearsay" witness and in this way conformed to its own object, the crucified and risen Lord. Hearing the Easter predication concerning the Jesus who visibly died on the cross as one who is now risen and thus vindicated, indeed exalted to live and reign until all enemies of God are forever defeated, engages believers in their Lord's trial, stretched out between "the already" of Jesus's proclaimed resurrection and the "not yet" fulfilled promise of their own.

To ask for academic certainty regarding such theological assertion of the promise of God made in the purported resurrection of the crucified Jesus is a category mistake, unless it is asking for a different kind of certainty: the certainty of faith in a specific word of promise. In the latter case of certainty of faith the concern is for a knowable, identifiable promise in the world; theology is thus concerned with identifying Jesus of whom the Easter gospel speaks as the historically particular human being who he was and remains, in turn identifying God as the Father of this Son on whom the Spirit rests. Thus the point of Christian assertion of truth is not and cannot be to overcome the academic skeptic's uncertainty about a contingent truth of history, purportedly, yet also essentially, referring to something future and thus admittedly not yet visible. Quite the contrary, to remind that the Christian's certainty is not academic certitude but remains the certainty of faith which trusts a purportedly divine promise protects theology from the intellectual vice of dogmatism. Dogmatism would leave behind the scandal of the cross by taking the report of the gospel as a present-day fact for anyone to see—"evidence that demands a verdict," as grotesque apologetics claim. But such a verdict would not in any case be Christian faith, as Dietrich Bonhoeffer pointed out. Founding Christian faith on historical evidence to overcome the scandal of the cross and the risk of faith would only be belief in the evidence of one's own eyes. The sinful human self-reference remains intact, indeed reinforced and fortified. But this is Christian self-deception which fathers the degenerate form of theology which is fundamentalism's "God said it. I believe it. That settles it." "Yes, perhaps," Luther at his best would respond (at his worst, admittedly, he indulged himself in such obscurantism): "but did God say it to you? Do you understand it? Warrant your understanding! Show me your exegesis!"

Clarity about this peculiar vulnerability of theology is not a weakness, then, but truly a strength. To make a contemporary illustration: in post-Holocaust Jewish-Christian dialogue, it becomes clear today that the eminently reasonable Jewish objection to Christian faith in the crucified Messiah is that scripturally the Messiah is like Moses, Joshua, or David. That is to say, Messiah conquers the forces of evil and establishes righteousness on the earth. To predicate crucifixion of the Messiah of God, then, is a manifest contradiction. As we heard, it is like saying "Victor victimized"; such self-contradictory predication cannot but be nonsense, folly, and a stumbling block. To this objection, Luther's Pauline Christian must reply, "Precisely! But let me explain this rhetorical paradox—it is not nonsense but new language for the hitherto unimagined reality of the Lord who reigns by virtue of a self-giving act of love for the unworthy and inferior."

Such an account does not eliminate the riskiness of faith but certifies it, indeed intensifies it. In replying this way, the Christian, who asserts the now-by-faith and coming-to-be-seen Lordship of Jesus who was crucified, bears the cognitive cross of living, under prevailing appearances to the contrary, what faith believes, following Jesus in the Spirit through all the uncertainties of trial and testing in present, contested reality. Inasmuch as the distinction between appearance and reality is at the heart of all critical thinking, just this tension is what preserves Christian theology as a critical discipline. Doubt is part and parcel of faith because the certainty of faith never rests upon appearances which often contradict what is believed in Christian faith. The certainty of faith rather lies precisely in the experience of conflict with the way things are and appear to be—as Jürgen Moltmann's "theology of hope" has stressed in recent times. Consequently the vulnerable stance of the martyr, as Luther spells it out in his hymn text, *A Mighty Fortress*, is the Christian "orthopraxis" that corresponds to the vulnerable faith that "orthodoxy" intends. Whether and to what extent this orthopraxis is sustained in any already triumphant orthodoxy backed by political-coercive power is a burning question today at the "end of Christendom." In any case, if the proper ethical form of orthodoxy is witness (what the Greek word, *martyr*, originally meant), testimony, or confession, that is because its claim to truth points forward to the coming of God who alone demonstrates the truth of Christian-theological words about God in the eschaton of judgment.

It was not by accident, then, that the first public statement of church doctrine subscribed by Luther and his early followers at Augsburg in 1530 was titled a "confession"— echoing New Testament apocalyptic found in the statement of Jesus, "whoever confesses me before men, the Son of Man will confess before God when he comes in glory with his angels." The ecumenical intention of the Augsburg Confession was to articulate the Christian claim to truth in dispute with contemporary "papists"—the latter still a party position in 1530 distinguishable in principle from the Church of Rome. The ecumenical intention was spelled-out in the Augsburg Confession's Preface. The intention was to articulate justification by faith as the criterion, after the model of Paul's Letter to the Galatians,[5] for genuine church reform and renewed unity. That claim for justification by faith as the "rule" (Galatians 6:16) was executed in Article IV concerning justification: "human beings cannot be justified before God by their own powers, merits, or works. But they are justified as a gift on account of Christ through faith when they believe that they are received into grace and that their sins are forgiven on account of Christ, who by his death made satisfaction for our sins." Notably, this Spirit-given faith in Christ the Lamb of God bearing away the sin of the world also believes something about oneself, namely as received into grace and forgiven. It is this particular faith which personally appropriates the God-given righteousness who is Christ as given "for me" that God

---

5. Luther published an early (1519) and a later commentary on Galatians (1535). The later commentary is considered to be his mature statement on the doctrine of justification; see LW 26, 27.

"reckons" as righteousness.[6] Believing this object entails this self-involving subjectivity or else its genuine objectivity is not grasped at all.

Just as in Galatians, this ecumenical intention is set within the apocalyptic perception of a time of trial when confessors are called to the witness stand to make their testimony; the time for confession comes when the integrity of the church under the gospel is jeopardized. The timeliness of the act of confession is thus essential. If this setting in life is forgotten and left behind, the once-timely act of confession itself is transformed into something else—a supposedly timeless truth which can now act legally is a foundational document, like a constitution.

Historically, the Augsburg Confession quickly became such a legal document subscribed by ministers and leading laity, as local churches, which had adopted the reforms Luther advocated, sought legal recognition within the Holy Roman Empire. This new, legal use of the Augsburg Confession in emergent Lutheran confessionalism, fitting under the circumstances, is clearly derivative. Once this derivation is forgotten, it can actually obscure the root sense of confession as the vulnerable witness of a martyr to gospel truth under attack. Indeed, as the legal usage of the Augsburg Confession proceeded athwart the wide-ranging schisms of the sixteenth century, the question arises whether this legal usage in emergent confessionalism eclipsed the original situation of confession and thus transformed the vulnerable posture of the martyr into the triumphant posture of those who claimed to have achieved orthodoxy as opposed to others. This anti-ecumenical eclipse and its accompanying recourse to state patronage, "Christian Republicanism" as John Witte Jr. has named it,[7] is the decisive

6. Kolb and Wengert, eds., *Book of Concord*, 41.
7. Witte Jr., *Law and Protestantism*.

step historically on the road to legally established, politically enforced Lutheranism as a rival version of Christendom, one among other contending Christian orthodoxies. As their respective theologies battled each other during the long night of the European wars of religion that followed, inadjudicable theological conflict in the name of religion did much to discredit Christianity and the discipline of theology in the minds of thinking people.

Crucial to see here theologically is that Lutheran confessionalism-on-the-way-to-orthodoxy almost imperceptibly transformed the question theology was answering from that of Jesus, "Who do you say that I am?" (confession) to quite another question, "Which of the rival churches is the true one?" (orthodoxy). Historically this devolution may have been inevitable, but the theological cost was dear.

One of the reasons that this devolution may have been historically inevitable is that from the beginning Luther intended the reform of Christendom, not its dismantling. "Christendom" was the political order in the West stretching back to Charlemagne in which Christianity was the legally recognized religion; indeed, membership in civil society depended on baptism. The intention to reform the received form of political Christendom was acted upon in the several years before the Augsburg Confession when Luther and faculty colleagues at Wittenberg undertook the traditional episcopal function of visitation of local congregations for the purpose of oversight (since the "prince-bishops" in their territories had sided with the "papists" against them, refusing to ordain their ministers). Undertaking the forfeited ecclesiastical ministry of oversight, this new performance of visitation was conducted with the support and at the command of the secular prince; the recommendations that resulted from the visit were likewise addressed to the secular authority, since in the framework of Christendom,

## LUTHERAN THEOLOGY

it was the prince who bore political responsibility for the temporal welfare of clergy and congregations.

This was not an unlikely development. Luther's intention to renew Christendom was already visible in his early treatise on the Babylonian captivity[8] of the church in which he appealed to the secular princes, as the responsible Christian laity with political jurisdiction, for thoroughgoing reformation of church and society. Although it grates on our ears after the democratic and egalitarian political evolutions of the modern Western world, this claim for the patronage of the temporal authorities joined seamlessly with Luther's teaching on the "priesthood of all believers," empowering the laity—in this case the laity who are the secular authorities. So the "priesthood of all believers" was the source both of a democratic and egalitarian fermentation in Western culture and at the same time gave birth to the remarkable subservience of Protestant churches to the early modern nation-state. What Quentin Skinner once summarized in regard to the Reformation under Henry VIII, "the Church *in* England became the Church *of* England" applies equally to the Lutheran territorial churches on the continent.[9] This commitment of the so-called magisterial Reformation to the reform of Christendom correlates with Luther and Lutheran theology's early rejection of both the revolutionary and pacifist wings of the Anabaptist movement. Rebaptism was murderously rejected, not least because it implied the invalidity of the church which had baptized infants and thus undermined the very foundation of Christendom.

What form should the discipline of theology take if the cultural task undertaken is to renew Christendom? Early Lutheranism saw two models emerge, though in truth the first of them harkened back to the time before the

8. Luther, *Babylonian Captivity of the Church*, LW 36:11–126.
9. Skinner, *Foundations of Modern Political Thought*.

conversion of Constantine when an unestablished church existed in a highly pluralistic religious environment and thus needed to discipline itself to endure with integrity. In response to the wretched condition of the churches that Luther witnessed during the visitation, he sought to revive the ancient Christian "Torah instruction" (on the model of the book of Deuteronomy) of catechesis. Luther's form of doctrinal or dogmatic theology is thus articulated as introductory explanation of Christian texts traditionally deemed indispensable for nurturing the conscientious life of the baptized believer. These indispensable texts he deemed to be in order: the Ten Commandments, the Apostles' Creed, the Lord's Prayer, Baptism, Confession, and the Lord's Supper. Thus Luther, rejecting the academic esotericism of medieval scholasticism, re-imagined the presentation and inculcation of Christian doctrine in a model that harkened back to the catechetical lectures of the church fathers, indeed further back to the book of Deuteronomy.

Simultaneously, however, Luther's younger colleague Philip Melanchthon devised an alternative model for dogmatics. He employed the "topical" method of humanist scholarship, a device for reading texts on their own terms by studying vocabulary and its various uses in context. Using this literary method, however, eventually became untenable because it presupposes the literary unity of the Bible, a presupposition undermined in time by far more careful and exacting study. Even so, Melanchthon still needed a scheme with which to outline and organize an almost infinite number of available topics from the many discrete entries in the canonical Scriptures. For this purpose, Melanchthon utilized Paul's Letter to the Romans—thus making it the Lutheran "canon within the canon." Under topical headings taken in sequence from Romans, he gathered evidence from the rest of the Bible in support of a fulsome treatment of such topics as creation, image of God, sin, promise and faith, law and gospel and so on. Largely it was Melanchthon's model, supplemented by renewal of the method of academic disputation that had been honed in medieval scholastic theology, which was followed in the self-consciously academic theology of Lutheran Orthodoxy. This deductive methodology has its own hidden but vulnerable presuppositions, yet from the beginning it predominated in Lutheran Orthodoxy. This predominance of the topical method happened, not only because Melanchthon was the primary author of the texts of Lutheran confessionalism (especially the Augsburg Confession and its Apology) but also because after Luther's death it was his students who consolidated early Lutheran Orthodoxy in the 1580 Formula of Concord.

Following the topical method and renewing the disputatious form of argumentation from the medieval tradition, the Formula of Concord sought to resolve dangerous contentions within early Lutheranism; it thus inaugurated the theology of Lutheran Orthodoxy. In doing so, however, its consolidation of early Lutheranism came at the ecumenical cost of anathematizing not only the Church of Rome but also the Reformed Protestantism that crystallized around the legacies of Zwingli and Calvin. Neither of these anathematizations were without precedence in Luther himself. His attack on the papal "antichrist" is well-known and was included in the Lutheran confessional writings in his Smalcald Articles. But already Luther had disputed christologically with Zwingli, as we have seen; by 1580 the christological dispute initiated in the controversy over the Lord's Supper had enlarged to encompass the difficult but also decisive doctrine of divine election or "predestination."

How so? Is Christ merely God's "second thought," that is, an ex post facto reaction to unanticipated human sin? If not, is Christ then instrumental to a prior and absolute decree of God which determines from eternity the fate of all things, thus also the divine election of some from an equally willed damnation of most humanity? So the teaching of the Reformed appeared to the early Lutherans. Not only did the Reformed limit what for the Lutherans was the universal scope of Christ's atoning work to a select number of a predetermined elect; in the process it also subordinated the work and person of Christ to God, not taken essentially as the father of this son but as the Absolute. The very being of God was not strictly conceived according to the relational ontology of the doctrine of the Trinity, as the Father of his beloved Son on whom he breathes his Spirit, but rather absolutely as sheer arbitrary and omnipotent will—a conception which tended toward the Arian heresy of an un-trinitarian Unitarianism (doctrinal deviations which actually afflicted early Calvinism). The early Orthodox Lutheran rejection of the Reformed doctrine of double predestination was articulated in the Formula's final Article XI.

Article XI's affirmation of universal atonement, however, seemed to imply universal salvation, an inference which the early Lutherans quickly rejected. Rather, it seemed to them as it also had to Melanchthon that there must be some reason in humans for their damnation in spite of the universality of Christ's atonement. In the course of time, then, this rejection of universal salvation tended to reintroduce the human will as a small but crucial factor separating the sheep from the goats. Already Melanchthon indicated that the willingness to accept Christ as Savior not only differentiated the elect from the reprobate but caused that differentiation. Thus the problem of "cheap grace" semi-Pelagianism, which had so provoked Luther's initial attack on the optimistic anthropology of late medieval scholastic theology, returned through the back door into Fortress Lutheranism.

Unsurprisingly, the rejection of double predestination also came at the cost of a certain incoherence with the teaching of Luther, well-known from his treatise on bound choice, as previously discussed. Luther toyed in the treatise against Erasmus with a notion of double-predestination as something suggested by the hiddenness of God that remains as a dark penumbra backgrounding the light of grace, something only to dissipate at last in the fulsome light of glory. It is interesting to observe how Luther pinpointed the darkness attending even the revealed God of grace: just as for the Reformed, for Luther God apparently elects some to faith but passes over others. But this perception is qualified by Luther as one made according to the human experience of Christians in the present time when we see but through a glass darkly. Decisively, it remains to be seen what will become of others to whom faith has not presently been granted, in the meantime believing in the righteousness of God revealed in Christ. Of course, great ambiguity remains here. Does Luther mean that believers will rejoice to see the now manifest justice of the damnation of those to whom faith is withheld? Or does Luther hint that believers will be surprised at how many of the apparently faithless will accompany them in glory?

Without expressly saying so, in his bold speculation about the dark God "hidden in majesty" as opposed to the bright shining God "revealed in manger and cross," Luther at least verbally endorsed the Arian heresy, that is, the speculation about an absolute God "not bound to his word" as father is bound to son. Upon critical reflection, Luther's experimentation with this Arian thought makes manifest what is the cost of an unbaptized theism[10] over against the Christian

10. Jenson, *Unbaptized God.*

faith in the Almighty Father who is eternally the father of his own son, Jesus Christ the savior of sinners, as the unleashed Holy Spirit gives faith where and when he wills. In that case the scope and power of the atoning work of the Son is understood as equal to the infinitely creative work of the Father, as believers are reminded they ever remain at the mercy of the Spirit. "As you believe so you have," Luther was wont to say. As the objectivity of faith is given in the person of Jesus Christ, the Son of God, it is accessed by the personal work of the Holy Spirit who makes a theological subject by the gratuitous grant of faith, constituting a new human person. If this is the case, it follows that if and when faith relapses from grace into the mere light of nature, it cannot but speculate about a God "not bound by his word."

Historically speaking, entertaining this Arian thought had been enabled by the nominalist theology of late scholasticism in which Luther had been trained. Occam distinguished between the absolute and the ordered power of God in such a way that whatever God apparently ordains can without contradiction be overruled at any moment by God's absolute power so that whatever God wills must necessarily take place—even if it contradicts the ordered will of God as it appears in revelation. Ostensibly concerned to protect the freedom of God from metaphysical capture, Occam's distinction actually untethered the trinitarian correlation of divine freedom with wisdom and love. From now on, it was power and power alone that made God God in the minds of theologians. Years after the polemic against Erasmus, Luther expressed regret over this speculative line of thought and his own rhetoric concerning "the necessary foreknowledge of God" in the treatise; he insisted now instead that Jesus Christ names God in God's absolute power as the Father of all mercies and the God of all consolation.[11] Hidden in

11. Kolb, *Bound Choice*.

the voluminous Genesis lectures, this retraction was little-known; consequently Reformed theologians subsequently could wave Luther's text on bound choice in the face of the latter-day Orthodox Lutherans and maintain that they were better followers of Luther than they.[12]

The Formula of Concord negotiated a number of disputes among German Lutherans that arose in the time after Luther's death. These disputes, in addition to the one over election and free will just discussed, concerned original sin, the righteousness of faith and its relationship to good works, the proper distinction of law and gospel and the question about the law's abiding significance for the justified sinner, the Lord's Supper and the person of Christ and what he worked by his descent to hell, Christian freedom but also the obligation openly to confess in times of trial. All of this material in the Formula is materially interesting and exemplary in terms of clarity of argument, achieving terminological precision according to the scholastic method of patient disputation. This procedure displayed the intellectual virtues of the scholastic method of medieval academic theology. Combining this expertise with the new literary tools of humanism, the second-generation Lutheran theologians trained by Melanchthon were able to consolidate theologically the various Lutheran factions—one scholar has shown that in the interim between the Augsburg Confession and the Formula of Concord at least five different versions of the doctrine of justification by faith competed with each other among self-identified Lutherans![13] This consolidation defined the boundaries of what would become Orthodox Lutheranism. Yet here too the resolutions achieved came at some cost.

12. Raitt, *Colloquy of Montbeliard*.
13. Vainio, *Justification and Participation in Christ*.

For example the dispute over original sin decided against the position of a radical follower of Luther, Mathias Flacius, who held that after Adam's fall the very substance of humanity became sin. Theologically, this seemed not only to abolish the good creation of God abiding in depraved humanity after the fall, but in the process to destroy the basis for moral culpability, Adam's fall into sinfulness notwithstanding. The position seemed virtually Gnostic or Manichaean. It had to be rejected theologically in order to state that it is precisely God's good and highest creation in humanity which has fallen into sin and thus into a deeply dehumanizing captivity. When Flacius maintained that the substance of humanity had become sin, he re-introduced the binary Aristotelian technical terminology of "substance" as opposed to "accident." When the Formula, ruling against him, affirmed that the human substance remains God's good creation in relationship to which sinfulness is an accident, the Aristotelian thesis lived on in the Formula of Concord's antithesis.

Distinguishing the good substance of fallen humanity from the accidental quality of sinfulness acquired in the fall, however, inevitably minimized the breadth and depth and height of sinfulness by categorizing it as a mere accident of history which left the good substance of humanity untarnished. Thus the binary conceptual distinction from Aristotle between substance and accident reappeared, even though Luther had repudiated it with regard to the eucharistic doctrine of "transubstantiation" (which taught that that while the accidental appearance of bread remains, the underlying substance of bread is changed into the substance of the body of Christ). Thus, the substance-accident scheme was now not only reintroduced into the theology of Orthodox Lutheranism but claimed pride of place as providing a conceptual solution to a vexing controversy.

An even more fateful example of the deep perplexities into which Lutheran Orthodoxy fell with the Formula of Concord came with its resolution of a dispute stemming from the teaching of another disciple of Luther, Andreas Osiander. He drew on some of Luther's own rhetoric about the divine righteousness of the incarnate son of God swallowing up sin, analogized to a drop absorbed in an ocean. Taking this metaphor in a one-sided way, Osiander taught that justification occurred by the oceanic infusion of divine righteousness into the soul swallowing up and dissolving its sinfulness. The liquid metaphor of "infusion" could also appeal to Augustine's interpretation of his favorite verse in connection with justification in Romans 5:5 about God's love has been poured—like a liquid—into our hearts by the Holy Spirit. Osiander's retrieval of the infusion metaphor from the patristic and medieval heritage seemed especially wrongheaded to the followers of Melanchthon, for it seemed to undermine the objectivity of justification as the work and gift of Christ external to the self; in place of referring the believer to Christ she was directed to her own experience of God's love within for assurance of her status as a beloved child of God.

"Infusion" was also too close for comfort to the rival "papist" scheme in which the sacraments operated mechanically to dispense divine grace like a medical potion, injecting divine charity into sinful souls progressively to purify them, apart apparently from the individual's personal repentance and faith. They also detected in Osiander a christological view according to which abstract incarnation as such—sheer contact between intrinsic divine righteousness and accidental human sinfulness—constituted the saving act of God in Christ. This seemed to make Christ's incarnate life of obedience nugatory, a mere outward manifestation of an inner and prior state of being.

Further implications were deleterious: a solely incarnational interpretation of salvation could in principle employ any of the three divine persons for incarnation (modalism) and equally employ any finite creature as its materialization (docetism). Thus the saving righteousness of God was interpreted as an intrinsic divine property rather than the achievement of the obedient Son whose particular historical life mattered; this Christology overlooked the cross and especially the Gethsemane prayer of the incarnate Son on which Christian salvation truly depends.

Penitent sinners are rather sought and found by the saving righteousness of the particular Christ who is Jesus, Son of his Abba Father, as their Spirit proclaims this very event of his coming in the flesh as good news. This is an event of righteousness; it is not something naturally possessed by virtue of his divine nature alone, but rather is something achieved by this divine person's incarnate life, death and resurrection. And if saving righteousness on behalf of the ungodly is the personal work of the one Jesus Christ the Son of God and as such properly belongs to him alone, it is and ever remains "alien" to the believer to whom it is attributed as a gift through proclamation, not infused by means of a ritual working mechanically (Latin: *ex opere operato*).

Yet here as well the correction of Osiander's teaching by the Formula of Concord came at a cost—the cost of explicitly repudiating the allegedly imprecise language of the Augsburg Confession and its Apology from fifty years before. These seminal texts, following Luther's own usage just as Osiander had, regularly characterized justifying faith as "regeneration"—employing the biblical metaphor of the new birth. Indeed, an honest reading of the early Melanchthon, let alone Luther can hardly deny that they interpreted the biblical metaphor of the new birth precisely as the gift of justifying faith by the ministry of the Holy Spirit. How else could they maintain the "grace alone" in "faith alone" except by maintaining that Spirit-wrought faith comes upon one as a gift, even against one's will, as happened to Paul the apostle on the road to Damascus?

Yet in place of this, the Formulators established a psychologically implausible but all the same dogmatically necessary "order of salvation" to nip Osiander's doctrine of infusion in the bud. Regeneration or the "effective" righteousness of God's new creation, they affirmed, strictly follows upon the initiating divine and extrinsic act of "forensic" justification—God the judge pronouncing his "not guilty" upon the sinner to whom Christ's righteousness has been credited when the sinner, recalling the gospel, willingly and earnestly accepts it for himself. Justification first—sanctification thereafter!

Here too, however, the cost proved painful in the long term. This scheme—(forensic) justification first, (effective) sanctification second—begged the question of how the unregenerate sinner comes to faith in the merciful righteousness of Christ. Notice how in this scheme the Holy Spirit disappears from the action accept as a gloss upon what is essentially a terrified and drowning sailor's natural reach for a life preserver. For the early Melanchthon and Luther, however, this question of how anyone could ever grasp Christ crucified as if a life preserver was not begged; for them the scandal of the cross cannot be overcome, or rather overlooked, this way. Surely Christ crucified looks more to the drowning sailor like a millstone to be hung around his neck than a life preserver! Instead their answer to a question that cannot be begged in theology can be seen in numerous passages in the Augsburg Confession and its Apology; it was the personal transformation to faith effected by the free and sovereign calling of the Holy Spirit through the gospel word which effectively generated holy

## From Confessionalism to Orthodoxy

faith in Christ as God's lamb given "for me," the sinner. The sailor has drowned by its baptism into Christ and from this tomb the Spirit calls forth a new creation.

Of course, in that case, if coming to faith is by the Spirit-effective coming of the gospel from outside of the self to the existing self in order to transform the self into a new creation, faith itself is "divine" and "holy." In other words, justifying faith is already "sanctification" and so the Formula's scheme, "justification first—sanctification thereafter," falls to pieces on a fatal contradiction. But to fend off the threat posed by Osiander's doctrine, Orthodox Lutheranism could not face up to this conundrum. In the course of time, consequently, insistence upon its order of salvation scheme had to eclipse the sovereign and initiating role of the Holy Spirit and open up in its place a little space for human free will and its actually decisive action, the sinner's "decision of faith," the sailor's grasp after a life preserver. Indeed, it was this little act of human will in turn which caused the sheep to be separated from the goats. Thus a kind of evangelical semi-Pelagianism emerged as Lutheran Orthodoxy broke down on its own internal contradiction.

Lutheran Orthodoxy was from the beginning beset with such incoherencies, but the reader would be left with a false and one-sided impression if the matter were left there. Ample resources for study of Lutheran Orthodoxy are now available to the English language world. Already in the nineteenth century, Heinrich Schmid[14] compiled into one volume the teachings of the Orthodox Lutheran theologians and this highly useful volume was subsequently translated into English. It can still be found but an updated edition and republication would be highly desirable. This would fit with the scholarly project begun in the work of Jacob Preus,[15] who

14. Schmid, *Doctrinal Theology*.
15. Chemnitz, *Two Natures*.

translated important works of the "second Martin," Martin Chemnitz, who authored much of the Formula of Concord. Jacob's brother, Ralph Preus, produced a two-volume work on the theology of Lutheran Orthodoxy.[16] More recently, the voluminous *Theological Commonplaces* of the premier theologian of Lutheran Orthodoxy, Johannes Gerhard, are being translated into English.[17] These resources now available call for a deeper appreciation as well as a more precise critique of the theology of Lutheran Orthodoxy. We can only provide a sampling of that kind of engagement in what follows.

An interesting drama unfolded through the time of Lutheran Orthodoxy over the implications of Luther's apparent christological affirmation of the "ubiquity" (= "everywhereness") of the glorified body of the risen Christ. It should be noted from the outset that Luther affirmed the ubiquity of the body of Christ only hypothetically; his actual point seems to have been that the body of Christ can be everywhere and anywhere but it is certainly there where Christ has freely promised to meet believers, that is, as they gather in holy communion—the Pauline *koinonia* of his body and blood. Were there such a hypothetical fusion of natures in Christ, as the affirmation that Christ's finite body has become omnipresent would seem to require, it would dissolve the human nature into the infinity of God, producing de facto a heretical "monophysite" or "docetic" representation of Christ. From this it would follow that the incarnate Christ would be present everywhere naturally and, to boot, *as* his personal promise, just as God is omnipresent by nature, automatically as it were.

Such "Christopanism," so to speak, was *not* Luther's intention; he drew back from this evident implication already during the controversy with Zwingli by making the

16. Preus, *Theology of Post-Reformation Lutheranism*.
17. Gerhard, *Theological Commonplaces*.

following distinction: "It is one thing if God is present and another if he is present *for you*."[18] Or again, "both God and Christ are not far away but near, and it is only a matter of revealing themselves . . ."[19] But to be reveal oneself for the sake of another is a free act of personal will. Luther's subtle distinction here will prove important, because by virtue of this distinction between what is true by nature and what is true personally, the bodily presence of the risen Christ "for us and our salvation" remains subject to the personal will of the one Jesus Christ, the Son of God.

It is not as though by virtue of his resurrection, or by virtue of the true divinity of the divine Son in its personal union with human nature and the communication of their respective properties with one other in the incarnation and mission of redemption, that Christ's body is, as it were, naturally and impersonally distributed to every nook and cranny of the universe. This apparent implication is that to which opponents, especially in Reformed circles, took exception. They, by contrast, confined Christ's finite body to a locally conceived "heaven" somewhere up above and thus spoke of the Spirit lifting believers up to Christ in the Lord's Supper. While this affirmation of the Spirit's role in raising believers in faithful anticipation of their heavenly destiny in Christ is to be appreciated, as a counter position to perceived Lutheran ubiquitism it is not without its own problems, especially that of conceiving of heaven as a local place above the clouds. In any case, the apparent implication of Luther's affirmation of the risen Christ's bodily presence was the objectionable notion that Christ's human body was thereby dissolved into divine omnipotence. The human body stretched to infinity is no longer human or a body! Luther's teaching was yet another kind of monophysitism.

18. LW 37:68.
19. LW 37:66.

In response, Chemnitz clarified Luther's speculative exploration of the deity's "repletive presence" (divine immensity or omnipresence) as a property communicated to the glorified Christ as the condition for the possibility of Christ's promised eucharistic presence. To substantiate Luther's distinction here, Chemnitz robustly re-introduced the trinitarian nature-person distinction and accordingly spoke of the *ubivolipraesens* (presence-where-he-wills) of Christ,[20] i.e., that Christ the divine-human *person* is present for others as he *freely* wills to be. Moreover, he is personally present as truly he is, as the body once broken but now glorified for us.[21] With this move, Chemnitz was correcting Melanchthon in Luther's direction. Fearing the heretical confusion or mingling of divine and human natures proscribed by the Fourth Ecumenical Council at Chalcedon, Melanchthon in the time between Luther and the Formula of Concord had already retreated from Luther's doctrine of the communication of idioms in the personal union. For the mature Melanchthon, Luther's daring ascription of human suffering to the divine Son of God incarnate is only a way of talking, not of a true way of being.[22] But this turns Luther on his head. For Luther, there can only be a way of truly talking about Christ if it is talking truly of his way of being. Melanchthon's distinction is, in Luther's perspective, a relapse from theology into philosophy. In philosophy, critical thinking separates the sign from the thing signified, the way of talking from the way of being. But in theology critical thinking unites the sign and the thing signified: Jesus *is* the Son of God. This loaf *is* his body.

---

20. See, e.g., Chemnitz, *Two Natures*, 278.

21. On this point, see further Hinlicky, "Luther's Anti-Docetism," 139–85.

22. On this, see further Hinlicky, *Paths Not Taken*, 162–69.

Thus following Luther, Chemnitz held that properties of the divine nature are truly communicated to the human nature so that it is possible with Luther to say that "This Body gives life" or "This Man is omnipresent" or conversely that the Son of God hungers, thirsts, and is abandoned to death by God, his Abba-Father. As mentioned, Luther's seemingly unqualified speech in this fashion was controversial and given to misunderstanding in its time, but in Chemniz it is qualified by the personal will of Christ, so that it will be more precisely stated, This Body gives life where and when its Head wills and promises; this Man is definitely and personally present where and when the Son of God wills and promises; this Son of God suffers and dies in true obedience to God his Father.

Broadly speaking, the development of Orthodox Lutheran Christology following Chemnitz retrieves the work of the church father, Cyril of Alexandria, who battled against the Nestorian Christology of "two sons"—one of Mary and the other of God—albeit, in close proximity, "an indwelling" of the Son of God in the son of Mary. Drawing upon Cyril, Chemnitz writes: "Christ, according to His human nature and insofar as this nature is personally united with the Logos, differs from the other saints not only by reason of His gifts, which by comparison excel the others in number and degree, but also by reason of the union He differs totally from the saints."[23] The person of Jesus Christ the Son of God is the mysterious-miraculous personal union of the sign (the man born of Mary who suffered under Pontius Pilate) and the thing signified (the eternal Son of God); this union and its human perception is a "mystery" given to faith by the divine work of the Holy Spirit. Precisely as miracle, accordingly,

23. Chemnitz, *Two Natures*, 263. For a more detailed treatment of Chemnitz and Gerhard in Luther's christological legacy from which this discussion is drawn, see Hinlicky, *Beloved Community*, 509–36.

this person is not a fact of history there for anyone to see but must be revealed in a corresponding transformation of human subjectivity. All that is seen naturally is the sign. The unification of the sign and the thing signified for someone to apprehend remains the sovereign and personal work of the Spirit freely given where and when it pleases God. Correspondingly, the self-donation of the Son of God in the incarnation and henceforth as the risen body and soul of Jesus in the Lord's Supper is the free act of the person; so he is there for us as he wills and promises, namely in the holy communion of the church in mission to the nations. Otherwise Chemnitz writes, citing John of Damascus against the Nestorians, one actually makes "the union into something temporary and a matter of indwelling, as when God dwells in the saints."[24] Consequently the saving miracle of the person of Jesus Christ is obscured as also the present event of his self-revelation in the breaking of the bread.

Tacitly, it is a certain ("social") version of the doctrine of the Trinity that makes it possible for Chemnitz cogently to refute those who falsely "assert that the force of the term, *koinonia,* communion or communication, lies in the fact that whatever is said to be communicated becomes in itself a proper, essential, formal, subjective, or inherent part of that to which it is said to be communicated." Communication is not substantial metamorphosis; it is a social event of sharing, not a physical or metaphysical change from one kind of substance into another. In Christology, the *communio idiomatum* is a personal and so free communication by the divine Person of the eternal Son who is the one and only agent (and "patient!") of the Incarnation. Just so, the communion "by no means includes or implies in its meaning

---

24. Chemnitz, *Two Natures,* 264.

a conmingling, conversion, abolition, or equating" of the natures, human or divine.[25]

Chemnitz's quiet polemic here is aimed at the idea of a rival early Lutheran theologian, Johannes Brenz, who took Luther's speculative discussion of ubiquity to mean that the communication of idioms is not a personal action of the divine Son's free obedience to his divine Father in the act of assuming human nature in the mission of redemption. Rather for Brenz the communication of natures is itself the Incarnation, which can thus be and actually came to be viewed as a dynamic exchange-event occurring universally. Beginning with the post-enlightenment German philosopher George Friedrich Hegel (in fact a descendent of Brenz), significant modern Lutherans have thought this to be the real fruit of Luther's christological innovation. But here, in notable contrast to Luther, philosophical comprehension grasps the real meaning of theology's mere representations of crucified God and exalted humanity. Speculative, so-called "cosmic" Christologies draw from this inspiration a kind of Christopanism ever more remote from the flesh and blood reality of Jesus. The cost of this move, however, is displacement of the mediating notion of free personal agency and with it the "social" tri-personhood of the Father, the Son, and the Holy Spirit in the doctrine of the Trinity which it presupposes.

In any case, Brenz's christological view seemed to open a path to a far more radical affirmation of God's capacity for suffering—an affirmation which could also appeal to statements of Luther. If the human properties are also communicated not merely to the divine person of the Son but to the divine nature, then the personal statement, "The Son of God suffered in the flesh," is transposed into an ontological statement regarding pathetic divine nature

25. *Theological Commonplaces*, 309.

itself. Thus we can say: "God died on the cross." The implication is an ontology that would have to account for a true, albeit divine way of suffering or, more radically, even perishing in the sense of going out of existence. Many critics (Thomists of varying persuasions) of Hegel and some champions of him (like Slavoj Žižek) have seen in this affirmation of divine pathos a slippery slope to post-Christian atheism: the abstract otherworldly God died when no one came to rescue Jesus on the cross; but his militant spirit lives on in revolutionary movements.

No one in the epoch of Lutheran Orthodoxy worked through these difficulties in Christology with such acumen as did Johann Gerhard who pushed the argument forward to see that Luther's christological affirmation fairly begged for a concurrent retrieval of a more social doctrine of the Trinity then was customary in the Latin West. The Eastern trinitarian distinction between nature and person[26] is raised up from the outset of his christological presentation and made its linchpin: "The confusion of this distinction in this article is the target against which all heretics once struck."[27] While the term, "nature," designates the "essence" or the definition of a thing and may be contrasted with "existence" as possible contrasts with actual, in this latter connotation of actual existence a "nature" is virtually identical to "hypostasis" as the specific way that any "nature" is actualized in its existence.

As perhaps we better see today in hindsight: the important point here is that "nature" as such has no real existence; it is only a concept which works semantically to classify sets of characteristic possibilities for the efficient sorting of information about really existing things and persons. What actually exists are such hypostases that in

26. See Meyendorff, *Byzantine Theology*, 180–81.
27. Gerhard, *Theological Commonplaces*, 38.

turn are always specific concrete ways of being in a world. Hence "the hypostasis of the Son and His divine nature do not differ in reality,"[28] since Sonship is his way of being in the divine and eternal Trinity. Moreover, hypostasis, as the specific actualization of an abstract set of possibilities, yields a specific "characteristic, by which a person in the Godhead is distinguished from the other persons inwardly, and it is [thus] supremely proper to each person."[29] So the Father is God but in the way of being a father; the Son is God but in the way of being a son; and the Spirit is God but in the way of being the spirit of the Father breathed upon the Son. So "God" does not "exist" except as the Father, the Son, and the Holy Spirit, who each instantiate "God" personally, albeit only together in eternal communion of love with one another.

Thus between these persons, as Gerhard writes, there is an eternal and "essential communication."[30] All that the Father has and possesses as true God—that is to say, all divine possibilities other than the Father's concrete way of being as the unoriginated origin in the divine life—are generated as the Son and breathed as the Spirit and thence acknowledgment is returned in the personal loving praise of the Son in ecstasy of the Spirit to the source, God the Father. This essential communication is the dynamic circulation of divine life (as in a dance; Greek: *perichoresis*). This eternal and essential communication is proper to God and strictly speaking incommunicable, as it simply is the eternal life that God alone is. Human beings come to participate "proximately and spiritually" in the divine nature as creatures. *Theosis* (Greek: deification) is a personal and creaturely participation in the eternal life of the Three, not

28. Meyendorff, *Byzantine Theology*, 162.
29. Meyendorff, *Byzantine Theology*, 172.
30. Gerhard, *Theological Commonplaces*, 273.

the natural fusion of humanity and deity, which would be an impersonal absorption into the ocean of divinity.[31] That being said, the divinization of creatures in the gift of eternal life is the very goal of the Trinity: "The redemption of the human race includes not only privative goodness—that Christ freed us from sin, the wrath of God, from death and hell—but also positive goodness, that He brought us to perfect righteousness, the grace of God, the gift of the Holy Spirit, and eternal life."[32]

All this bears directly on Christology, in that "the Son of God assumed the human nature so that in and with it He might perform the office of mediation, redemption and salvation" and thus communicated to his own humanity whatever divine powers were requisite to performing the "prophetic, priestly and royal office."[33] This assumption of humanity is and ever remains the personal work of the second trinitarian person, the Son of God, by which the Son's "natural properties" as God are communicated to the assumed humanity not, so to say, *carte blanche* but as needed for the performance of the messianic office committed to the Son in the eternal self-determination of the Trinity to create, redeem, and fulfill our world. In this way Gerhard carefully fends off the Brenzian rendering of Christology, amounting to a confusion of natures, by advocating a Christology that accentuates the unique and personal union of natures.

As Wesley Hill has recently shown with regard to the sources of Christology in the Apostle Paul,[34] the Philippians 2 journey of the Son of God in the narrative of his humiliation and exaltation by which the Messianic office of redemption

31. Gerhard, *Theological Commonplaces*, 220, cf. 267.
32. Gerhard, *Theological Commonplaces*, 138.
33. Gerhard, *Theological Commonplaces*, 266.
34. Hill, *Paul and the Trinity*.

is accomplished can be articulated against a characteristic Western choice posited between "high" and "low" Christology—as if the point of Christology were to register on a high-low spectrum the degree of divinity attributed to the creature Jesus. One then either affirms abstractly and absolutely that Jesus is God (the modalist error of Marcellus of Ancyra which erases the personal distinction of the Father and the Son), as if sheer contact of divine to human were the gospel as such, or in reaction against this, one denies this bad Christology as a parochial Christian idolatry, but at the cost of denying the Son's true divinity (the error of Arius which makes the Son a second, created God).

But the personal union is and remains the personal act of the particular person, the Son of God sent by the heavenly Father and endowed with his Spirit. It is not an "essential union"[35] which, as Gerhard points out following Chemnitz, would have to be some sort of "physical transfusion and subjective inhesion" of divine properties in the human nature.[36] But adhering carefully to the gospel narrative allows Gerhard instead to affirm that just as "Christ did not have a glorified body until in His state of exaltation after the resurrection, so also He did not have a glorified soul perfectly endowed with angelic gifts until in His state of exaltation," thus allowing for the true finitude, the growth and indeed ignorance of the assumed soul.[37]

Despite internal contradictions inherited from the beginning, at its best Lutheran Orthodoxy retrieved patristic Christology in such a fashion that it made clear the interdependence of what Reformation theology wanted to say about the saving work of the one person Jesus Christ the Son of God and the robustly trinitarian understanding of the

35. Gerhard, *Theological Commonplaces*, 272.

36. Gerhard, *Theological Commonplaces*, 260–61.

37. Gerhard, *Theological Commonplaces*, 286.

divine reality. While this legacy would continue as a minority report within the theology of liberal Lutheranism in the nineteenth century, as we shall see, it has increasingly gained traction through the course of the twentieth century.

Yet there was also a minority report within the epoch of Orthodoxy, once again attesting to internal contradictions going back to the beginning: Pietism. Lutheran theology in the early modern period of late Orthodoxy was characterized by a peculiar polarization between an affective "theology of the heart"[38] over against the rationalistic theology of the inerrant Bible in Protestant Scholasticism. The rationalistic theology of biblical inerrancy knew a priori that a perfect being must manifest in the perfect revelation perfectly recorded therefore as an inerrantly inspired book. As this dogmatism increasingly gave way to the rise of critical biblical scholarship, as we shall see in the next chapter, the rationalism nevertheless lived on in a new form. The Enlightenment condemned the "enthusiasm" of the Pietists and produced a rationalistic philosophical theology "within the limits of reason alone," what Immanuel Kant finally named "ontotheology."[39] Given these choices and looking back, the liberal Lutheranism of the nineteenth century would ask polemically, "Which is Luther's true legacy?" Albrecht Ritschl's voluminous nineteenth-century study of Pietism sought to answer that leading question by delegitimizing Pietism's Lutheran credentials.[40] Ever since the Pietist movement has been subject to widely varying interpretations, as Pietist or Rationalist played surrogate in a convoluted debate about who truly inherited Luther's mantle in the age of rationalism. It is necessary here to

38. Cambell, *Religion of the Heart*, 2–3; Hinlicky, "Reception of Luther," 540–50; and Hinlicky, "Irony of an Epithet," 302–15.

39. Kant, *Lectures on Philosophical Theology*, 37–39.

40. Ritschl, *Three Essays*, 76.

make a brief detour into this maze of historical scholarship in order properly to assess Pietism.

Ritschl portrayed Pietism as spiritually egoistic, "world-denying" and thus a foreign development on the soil of Luther's reformation, a recrudescence of the medieval ascetic and mystical spirituality of "monastics who live a life free from cares" by flight from the world for the sake of private ascent to God. How different from the socially responsible "protestant Christians who remain within the midst of their secular conditions of life and who must stand the test of their faith within the inescapable cares of those conditions[!]"[41] But Heiko Oberman, who has done so much to relocate Luther within his actual historical context of late medieval Catholicism,[42] argued that the medieval "mystical" legacy is integral to Luther's "chief" doctrine: "If future research confirms my suggestions that Luther's concept 'extra nos' [outside the self] is related to [mystical] *raptus* [rapture], one of the major arguments for a forensic interpretation of Luther's doctrine of justification has been preempted. Though we have no claim to the *iustitia Christi* which is not our 'property' (*proprietas*), it is granted to us as a present possession (*possessio*). *Extra nos* and *raptus* indicate that the *iustitia Christi*—and not our own powers—is the source and resource for *our* righteousness. Epithets such as 'external' and 'forensic' righteousness cannot do justice to Luther's doctrine of justification."[43] Oberman's claim here has been extended in recent years by the Finnish scholar, Tuomo Mannerma[44] and his students,[45] though

---

41. Ritschl, *Three Essays*, 105.
42. Oberman, *Harvest of Medieval Theology*.
43. Oberman, *The Harvest of Medieval Theology*, 150–51.
44. Mannermaa, *Der im Glauben Gegenwaertige Christus*.
45. Saarinen, *Gottes Wirken auf Uns*.

others have independently made the same kind of critique of the Ritschl paradigm.

One effect of Oberman's historiography is to lend credence to the reclaiming of medieval spiritual theology by Johann Arndt (1555–1621) at the wellspring of Lutheran Pietism. Arndt did so on the model of Luther's own publication in 1516 and again in 1518 of a tract reputed to come from the school of John Tauler (1300–1361) under the title, *"German Theology."*[46] What is appropriated here in Arndt, as in Luther's precedent before him, and in Spener's afterwards,[47] is the theme of resignation, the Gethsemane of the soul, the *vita passiva* of the *theologia crucis*: "a pure simple suffering of the divine will; man allows God to work all things in him and does not hinder God with his own will or strive against God."[48] Thus, as Oberman wrote in the Preface to the English translation of Arndt's *True Christianity*: "Albrecht Ritschl was not completely wrong in tracing Arndt's lineage back to medieval and mystical traditions; it is the value judgment that went with Ritschl's work that deserves reconsideration . . . the learned theology of the schools was [to be] complemented by an affective theology accessible as well to the simple and unlettered." Indeed, Oberman claims, Arndt proves in this "to be a true disciple of Luther," a "second Luther, Luther *redivivus*," in articulating the paradox of the *simul iustus et peccator* precisely by means of the "mystical" rapture of encounter with the Christ who comes to unite with the self from outside of the self, as in Luther's celebrated "joyful exchange."[49] Luther's

46. LW 31:71–77.

47. Erb, trans., "Resignation," in *Pietists: Selected Writings*, 83–87.

48. Arndt, *True Christianity*, 30–31.

49. Oberman, "Preface," in Arndt, *True Christianity*, xvi. From the angle of Luther's trinitarianism, likewise, Gritsch concurs in this judgment: "Spener cited numerous texts from Luther and orthodox

own theology of "true faith, that gift of the Holy Spirit"[50] and of justification correspondingly as a "joyful exchange" at a wedding feast,[51] then, are indisputable sources of Pietism's Bridegroom of the Soul.

In an influential article published in the 1957 *Lutherjahrbuch*, Martin Schmidt did not reject, but sharply qualified the kind of continuity, for which Oberman later argued, from medieval spiritual theologians like Tauler and Bernard whom Luther knew and drew upon on through Arndt to later Pietists. He patiently dissected the relationship of justification and regeneration in the Pietists in terms of its more optimistic eschatology.[52] The theological innovation over against Luther was to regard sanctification as the possibility of optimistic living in this world after and on the basis of justification. Justification here becomes a past event, the believer's secured possession. God's free grace becomes a presupposition for what truly matters existentially, the believer's new life progressing forward. For the historical Luther, by contrast, the movement in Christian life remains the triune God's, the Spirit by the Word apocalyptically breaking into the closed system of this world as an incision to justify the ungodly who remain *simul iustus et peccator* until the eschaton completes God's radical surgery.

Schmidt's analysis, however, produces a quandary for theology in Luther's tradition. How could one ever adjudicate such a shift in horizon from the apocalyptic to progressive salvation history? Perhaps a deeper self-examination among those claiming Luther's mantel is required. F. Ernst

---

theologians that true theology could not be based on natural, rational power but only on the gift of the Holy Spirit." Gritsch, *History of Lutheranism*, 145.

50. LW 34:109.

51. LW 48:12–13.

52. Schmidt, "Spener und Luther."

Stoeffler pointed out that with Philipp Jakob Spener (1635–1705) "the reform party within seventeenth century Lutheranism had moved from sincere but indiscriminate criticism [as in Arndt] to a plan of action."[53] The programmatic action announced in Spener's *Pia Desideria* was the provocation that ignited conflict, since it implied that Luther's reformation itself needed reform. While Arndtian reform literature had been theologically challenged by Lutheran Orthodoxy from the beginning on its understanding of the relation of imputative justification to regeneration, it was acting on the Arndtian understanding of regeneration that threatened the hegemony of Lutheran Orthodoxy.

Bible study threatened the dogmatic method; small groups of laity gathered for prayer and edification threatened the rule of the clergy; and optimistic eschatology threatened Orthodoxy's closed-ranks battlefield mentality. For such reasons, Stoeffler observes, "the printed announcement of [Spener's] platform, which today seems so eminently sane, sensible and moderate, became the center of one of the most bitter theological debates in the history of Protestantism."[54] In some ways, the battle has never ceased. Stoeffler wondered whether there was a Lutheran contradiction at the root of the bitter incomprehension that arose between Orthodox and Pietist. He suggested that it was the doctrine of baptismal regeneration, quite in tension with Luther's notion of living, active, justifying faith. The inner contradiction virtually required an eventual parting of the ways.[55]

Generally speaking, the rivals, Pietism and Orthodoxy, have been seen on one side to represent real alternatives to one another, as in Ritschl's disciple, Ernst Troeltsch, who

---

53. Stoeffler, *Rise of Evangelical Pietism*, 235. See also Stoeffler, *German Pietism during the Eighteenth Century*, 7–23.

54. Stoeffler, *Rise of Evangelical Pietism*.

55. Stoeffler, *Rise of Evangelical Pietism*, 242.

disparaged a compromised, reactionary "church pietism" in favor of the rationalist critique of traditional theology and the ethical idealism of neo-Protestantism.[56] On the other side, these two apparent rivals have also been seen as siblings, kindred expressions of the same fundamental impulse, as in Karl Barth who detected the same titanism of "modern man" at work in both.[57] Broadly speaking, Barth had the deeper insight.[58] It is imperative to grasp this deeper unity of a shared modernist foundationalism in the age of Pietism and the Enlightenment. "Foundationalism" is the idea that philosophy can found the sciences on a secure basis with the meta-knowledge of knowledge, "epistemology." This foundational knowledge established by philosophy then serves as the "Tribunal of Reason" which rules in or out various disciplinary discourses as rational or irrational, as the case may be. Postmodernism today sees more clearly how this foundationalist endeavor attempted to overcome the radical historicity of human reason, thus corroborating Barth's insight into its "titanism." In such terms rival theologies of the heart and of the head appropriated Luther for their own foundationalist purposes, even if in either case they drew lines of continuity from Luther as well.

What Pietist and Rationalist indisputably shared was a changed historical horizon over against Luther. The historical Luther's horizon, as Heiko Oberman has demonstrated,[59] was an apocalyptic eschatology, requiring church and theology to keep "the gospel afloat in the world's last, ravaged hour."[60] But Pietist and Rationalist think quite otherwise about human prospects. The world has not ended; nature is

56. Troeltsch, "Leibniz und die Anfänge des Pietismus," 488–531.
57. Barth, *From Rousseau to Ritschl*, 44.
58. Busch, *Karl Barth and the Pietists*, 269–75.
59. Oberman, *Luther*.
60. Oberman, *Roots of Anti-Semitism*, 122.

opening up to scientific investigations. Commerce is bringing home the discovery of new peoples in new lands. Thirty Years of religious war had ceased. Hence, there is new hope in this world for this world, whether it be Spener's "better times for the church"[61] or Kant's dream of the maturation of the enlightened human race progressing onward towards perpetual peace. Accordingly, this epoch thinks in terms of "completing" the reformation of religion which Luther had begun with a reformation of Christendom.

Pietism's desire was to ground Christian faith in the *experienced* reality of the new birth; this may thus be seen as a kind of empiricist foundationalism within the more rationalistic milieu of the Continent, also if not especially in Lutheranism. Spener laid it down in his manifesto: "Hence it is not enough that we hear the Word with the outward ear, but we must let it penetrate to our heart, so that we may hear the Holy Spirit speak there, that is, with vibrant emotion and comfort feel the sealing of the Spirit and the power of the Word."[62] Luther can readily be quoted to the same effect and Spener did so—copiously. But the motives subtly diverge. The German scholar Rudolf Meyer called attention to this divergence between Luther and Spener's disciple, the leading Pietist theologian of his day, August Hermann Francke (1663–1727): "There is little in common between Francke's and Luther's experience of the religious crisis."[63] Luther sought assurance of grace as a troubled penitent. Francke as an orthodox Lutheran affirmed Luther's doctrine of grace. "But Francke had lost the

---

61. "Spener correctly sensed that the times had changed. The ministry of his day did not have to deal with people who wanted to be blessed from good works but with people who regarded them as unnecessary and impossible." Brown, *Understanding Pietism*, 107.

62. Spener, *Pia Desideria*, 117.

63. Meyer, *Leibniz*, 76.

immediate and personal experience of this love."[64] Study of Francke's account of his conversion makes it clear that his "religious dilemma becomes identical with an intellectual dilemma unknown to Luther." What was this new dilemma brought by the changed horizon of Enlightenment rationalism? "When, in his spiritual anguish, Francke turned to the Bible, it occurred to him 'to wonder whether the Scriptures are truly the Word of God. Do not the Turks make this claim on behalf of their Koran, and the Jews on behalf of the Talmud? And who shall say who is right?'"[65]

The early modern Pietist worries as much about historical relativism as about finding a gracious God. Francke's resolution of this worry is not cognitive; the rationalist objection is simply overwhelmed by the experience of the new birth: "So great was his fatherly love that he wished to take me finally, after such doubts and unrest of my heart, so that I might be more convinced that he could satisfy me well, and that my erring reason might be tamed, so as not to move against his power and faithfulness. He immediately heard me. My doubt vanished . . . I was assured in my heart . . . Reason stood away; victory was torn from its hands, for the power of God had made it subservient to faith."[66]

But how in the first place did this standoff between reason and feeling originate in the Lutheran theological tradition? As mentioned, as early as 1516, Martin Luther was deeply engaged in the reputed writings of the medieval mystic, Johannes Tauler (1300–1361).[67] Here he found a "critical alternative to the image of man in scholastic theology . . . insight into man's own inability and thus his

64. Meyer, *Leibniz*, 75.

65. Meyer, *Leibniz*, 75.

66. Francke "Autobiography," in Erb, trans., *Pietists: Selected Writings*, 105.

67. Brecht, *Martin Luther*, 137–39.

humble dependence on God."[68] During his student time at Wittenberg, Thomas Müntzer (1489-1525), of later notoriety for agitating the Peasants' Revolt, absorbed Luther's edition of (what was presumed to be Tauler's) *German Theology*. On Luther's recommendation, Müntzer became the preacher in Zwickau in 1520; there he met a layman, Nicolas Storch, who "possessed a remarkable knowledge of the Bible" but "emphasized special immediate revelations and illuminations." This claim to immediacy fascinated Müntzer; it was coupled with Storch's rejection of "special orders of ministers" and his initiation of "conventicles" to inspire true reformation. Untrained in theology, but believing "that he possessed the Spirit, Storch now developed a strong sense of mission and felt himself called to be a reformer of the church. One consequence in his circle was the rejection of infant baptism."[69]

After the radicalized Müntzer's departure from Zwickau, and while Luther was in hiding following the Diet of Worms, prophets from Zwickau under the leadership of Storch appeared in Wittenberg. From the distance of the Wartburg Castle, Luther urged his colleagues "to test the spirits"; but yet another coworker, Andreas Karlstadt (Luther's fellow professor at Wittenberg and partner at the Leipzig Debate against Johannes Eck), was captivated by the new prophesy. With two associates now lost, Luther wrote the 1525 polemical treatise, *Against the Heavenly Prophets*.[70] He linked Karlstadt's abandonment of his calling to theological scholarship to Storch's spell of prophetic immediacy, as if he could now "learn something better and more unusual

68. Brecht, *Martin Luther*, 142.

69. Brecht, *Martin Luther*, 36.

70. Luther, *Against the Heavenly Prophets in the Matter of Images and Sacraments*, LW 40:79-223.

than God teaches in the Bible,"[71] also then without the hard human work of scholarly theology. Martin Brecht observes: "Thus, for the first time, one of the difficult problems of the Reformation period was raised. The Bible and the office of preaching also were no longer regarded as means of obtaining the transcendent Spirit."[72]

Luther went on in the tract to articulate a doctrine of the *mediation* of divine revelation, the "external word" (*verbum externum*), a corollary of the teaching on justification, as we have heard, regarding the "alien" righteousness of Christ attributed as a gift to the sinner rather than acknowledged as his merited quality. This teaching was thus not simply a matter of the Bible's formal authority over against private interpretation or of learned hermeneutics over against reader-response speculation, though Luther makes such arguments. More profoundly, for Luther, the Word from God that matters tells a narrative and hence constitutes a unique and recognizable event; it comes as news from outside the self and as such meets and transforms the existing self, as it was figured, in giving *new birth*. The word that does this is not any word, not even any word in the Bible, but "the pure gospel, the noble and precious treasure of our salvation. This gift evokes faith and a good conscience in the inner man." Since the gospel's news of Christ's coming in mercy to befriend sinners is not innate, "outwardly [God] deals with us through the oral word of the gospel and the material signs" of Baptism and Supper. "Inwardly he deals with us through the Holy Spirit, faith, and other gifts . . . The inward experience follows and is effected by the outward . . . Observe carefully . . . this order, for everything depends on it."[73]

71. Luther, *Against the Heavenly Prophets*, LW 40:111.
72. Brecht, *Martin Luther*, 36.
73. LW 40:146.

In Luther's integration, then, the Spirit works *per Verbum*, by the Incarnate Word, thus as a *Verbum externum*, to give new birth as conformation to Christ's righteousness. The sequence is essential; it reflects the narrative structure of this new birth by which it is identified, recognized, and distinguished from imposters. If we "tear down the bridge, the path, the way, the ladder, and all the means by which the Spirit might come," we end up teaching "not how the Spirit comes to you but how you come to the Spirit." Or, what is the same, we give heed to some other spirit than the Spirit of Jesus and his Father and acquire some other righteousness than that which is properly Christ's. Such misunderstanding of the person and work of the Holy Spirit as someone or something other than the Spirit of Jesus and his Father is what Luther tagged as "enthusiasm" (the Greek word means literally "to be filled with a god") as if one had "devoured the Spirit"—as Luther wrote sarcastically thinking of the figure of the dove from Jesus's baptism, swallowing "feathers and all."[74]

Luther transposed the term into German as *Schwärmerei*. It denoted the same "self-delusion, a mistaken conviction that one had become a receptacle of a divine possession" as "enthusiasm." But in German *Schwärmerei* connoted "contagion and mass-frenzy," like "bees swarming around a hive," by which Luther could stigmatize his spiritualizing opponents, "the mobs that followed self-appointed field preachers or rampaged through churches, smashing the statues . . ."[75] Enthusiasm/*Schwärmerei* represents for Luther the wrong kind of integration of the Spirit—to the antecedent self, rather than to the Incarnate Word. Together Word and Spirit transform the antecedent

74. LW 83.
75. LaVopa, "Philosopher and the *Schwärmer*," 88.

self and thus form believers into the body of Christ and temple of the Holy Spirit.

Luther holds tightly together justifying faith or regeneration and the particular news of Christ's coming for those lost to God. He can hold them together because the Spirit who led Jesus in filial obedience and raised him from the dead is recognizably the same Spirit who raises those dead to God to new life by faith in his crucified and risen Son. In the ensuing centuries, however, Luther's sequenced integration of Word and Spirit was sundered in his would-be followers. Rival anthropocentric theologies "of the heart" and "of the head" eclipsed Luther's robust but often tacit trinitarianism[76] with different claims to "enlightenment"— also a kind of "new birth."

The metaphor of "enlightenment," to be sure, has a long history going back at least to Plato.[77] This makes claims for "the" Enlightenment of the modern West specious historically, as post-modern thought increasingly realizes. In the tradition of Augustinian theology to which Luther belongs, illumination (Latin: *illuminatio)* is the aforementioned work of the Holy Spirit, who bathes the transfigured Jesus in divine light, so that faith is born by this revealing-and-seeing-and-hearing of the Father's Son, Jesus who descends the mount to give his life for the many. Christine Helmer's pioneering analysis of Luther's trinitarianism[78] shows Luther at work with this Augustinian "enlightenment," the Spirit's attestation of the Word Incarnate at the Father's command, *Hunc audite* ("Listen to this One!") and just so bearing witness to those united with Jesus by faith that they too are children of God. Such "enlightenment" is at once intellectual and

76. Mauer, *Historical Commentary on the Augsburg Confession*, 239–70.

77. Plato, *Republic*, VI: 508–511; VII: 514–517.

78. Helmer, *Trinity and Martin Luther*, 230–70.

affective[79]—very much in contrast to "the" Enlightenment which principally pitted head against heart, duty against inclination, reason against affect, mind against body.

There is yet one more twist to the story. Luther's epithet, enthusiasm, suffered a strange reversal in the course of the Enlightenment. What happened historically is this: the Cartesian-Kantian ambition of clearly separating sensible and supersensible realms[80] predominantly worked to consign Luther's theological legacy to the company of the despised Pietists in a reactionary private realm of emotion where false, fervid imaginations—the unfounded source of all error—reigned unchecked. With no little irony and crowning this banishment, Luther's critique of enthusiasm could be retooled, no longer in service to the external word of the gospel but instrumentalized by the Tribunal of Reason to rule out gospel speech as irrational. In Kant's words from the Orientation essay: "Thus if it is disputed that reason deserves the right to speak first in matters concerning supersensible objects such as the existence of God and the future world, then a wide gate is opened to all enthusiasm, superstition and even atheism."[81] Indeed, as Kant's categorical claim indicates, the irony of Luther in the Enlightenment is that Luther's epithet, enthusiasm, was appropriated by the Tribunal of Reason to rule out of bounds Luther's own revelation-theology of the Spirit at work through external Word.[82] Thus rationalism could claim to have "fulfilled" or "completed" Luther's reformation, more consistently than Luther, albeit against his Christian intentions.

79. Hinlicky, "Luther's Anti-Docetism," 139–85.

80. Kant, "The Inaugural Dissertation," 188–93.

81. Kant, *Religion and Rational Theology*, 5.

82. See Kant, *The Conflict of the Faculties* 7.63, in *Religion and Rational Theology*, 283; and the discussion in Hinlicky, *Paths Not Taken*, 44–57.

# 3

# THE IDEALISTIC THEOLOGY OF LIBERAL LUTHERANISM

ONE CANNOT TELL THE tale about the rise of liberal Lutheran theology apart from its context in the "double crisis of modernity"—the background cultural narrative with which historian Robert Ericksen framed his important study of the failure of this iteration of Lutheran theology in his seminal *Theologians under Hitler*. The "double crisis" refers, first, to the undermining of the antecedent religion of Christendom—including its re-formation in Lutheran Orthodoxy—by the rationalist critique executed at the hands of the European Enlightenment; yet second, it refers also to the undermining of Enlightenment rationalism by the suspicious minds of the children of the rationalists: Marx, Nietzsche, and Freud. These rediscovered the historicity of reason and in a curious vindication of the Pietist theology of the affections, its subservience to desires of the heart of which enlightened Reason is innocently unaware. Even the putative deliverances of pure reason now fall under the suspicion of being self-justifying ideological formations rationalizing privilege vis-à-vis others, sinister purposes carefully concealed beneath a carefully crafted public persona. The intellectual and spiritual vertigo introduced by these successive deconstructions of antecedent civilizational certitudes played no little role in the rise of Hitler's National Socialism. Understanding this role helps to expose to understanding the baffling bewitchment that the Hitler cult worked on significant German Lutheran theologians in the '20s and '30s of the last century, including if not especially the self-proclaimed voices of "authentic Lutheranism."

Recently Christine Helmer has exposed the modern construction of the iconic Luther—not the historical Martin Luther, a medieval monk wanting to reform Christendom with all his "Catholic" baggage—but as a revolutionary reformer of religion as such whose breakthrough spoke across the centuries to contemporary Germans under the double crisis of modernity. This newly created heroic Luther articulated a religion of social conscience fully prepared for equally heroic sacrifice on behalf of the nation-state.[1] It was this new iteration of an ethically idealist Luther developed in the so-called "Luther Renaissance," engineered by the historical scholar Karl Holl on the heels of Adolf Harnack's deconstruction of the history of dogma, which prepared the ground for the conscientious German Lutheran decision for fascism.

It is notable already in this brief mention of the two major Lutheran figures at the climax of the epoch of liberal Lutheran theology how historians had eclipsed the dogmaticians of Orthodoxy. This reflects the fact that in liberal

1. Helmer, *How Luther Became the Reformer*.

## The Idealistic Theology of Liberal Lutheranism

Lutheran theology knowledge of God had been eclipsed by historical-critical knowledge of alleged knowledge of God. Pointing this out is hardly to sanction evasion of the modern critique of traditional theology as knowledge of God but to explore some ready but false responses to it for postmodern theology in the tradition of Luther. That is the task of this chapter.

A fuller account of this epoch would have to begin with a deep dive into the historical and naturalistic criticism of the Bible initiated in the early Enlightenment. For introductory purposes, however, here as elsewhere in this book we must be briefer. Baruch Spinoza, the Dutch Jew expelled from the synagogue for his heretical pantheism, spoke for his century when he wrote that it is not the Bible which interprets nature, but nature which interprets the Bible. "Being" or "the nature of things is not understood through the Bible, but the Bible itself is to be understood as a portion of this being, and therefore as subject to its general laws . . . The Bible is not the key to nature but part of it; it must therefore be considered according to the same rules as hold for any kind of empirical knowledge."[2] In this light biblical narrative does not say what actually happened; rather, the empirical discovery of what actually happened explains what the biblical text says.

In a time of interminable dogmatic disputes between the contending orthodoxies along with the bloody religious wars they fueled, this new and critical reading of the Bible had obvious appeal for defunding destructive fundamentalisms. Nor should it surprise at this point that it too could actually appeal to Luther who famously practiced a frank if primitive historical criticism. His work as a translator caused him to wrestle with the many perplexities and anomalies found in the canonical text such that if the divine

2. Cassirer, *Philosophy of the Enlightenment*.

purpose were to deliver a perfect book of perfect revelation reflecting the perfect being, the book we consequently got is rather a botched job. At the same time it was in this "manger" that Luther found the gift of the "Christ child." Precisely the clarity Luther acquired with his insight into the Word of God as the gospel proclamation for us of the resurrection of the crucified Jesus afforded him scholarly freedom from a biblicistic faith in the Bible as such. Luther does not believe in the Bible; he believes by means of the Bible.

Typically contemporary American religious culture poses an alternative between "literal" and "symbolic" reading of the Bible. Realizing in today's postmodernity, as we do, that human language is metaphorical "all the way down," this superficial binary sheds more heat than light. It doesn't help to sort things out much to say that biblical language about God is symbolic or metaphorical, when all human language about everything is symbolic or metaphorical. Suffice it to be said here that in terms of this contemporary American usage, Luther is no "literalist," though he insists upon the primacy of a literary reading of the Bible. Only a literary reading of the Bible can ascertain the reference of any given passage whether that be to some happening in human history or to the putative Author of history. Reference is what matters, since to make public sense one must know what in the world one is talking about; signs have significance as they point to something for auditors also to experience. Reference, however, is not literal representation nor does it depend on such; on the contrary, metaphors have reference and without discerning the reference one makes a hash too out of metaphors. To use Janet Soskice's humorous illustration: if I advise, "Don't touch the wire—it's live!" And you reply as you

## The Idealistic Theology of Liberal Lutheranism

grasp the wire, "Live wire? That's only a metaphor!"—you will be literally, not metaphorically, dead.[3]

Famously, as we have heard, and at a crucial point in his doctrine of Christ, Luther expressly denied the literal representation of the ascension of Christ to a local heaven somewhere above. Where Luther did take the Bible "literally" as representation, it was in want of alternative accounts of natural things such as the rise of modern science has provided. To such an extent is this true that it now fully informs the contemporary worldview. Just as contemporaries might be skeptical about cosmological speculations, say, about the so-called "multiverse," so the historical Luther was skeptical about Copernicus but also about Columbus's discovery of the New World across the Atlantic. Skepticism about speculations transgressing the limits of verifiable evidence is virtuous for the same intellectually conservative reason. In any case, for us still in the vertigo of the double crisis of modernity, the historical criticism of the Bible is an event that has taken place within theology just like Galileo's discovery of a heliocentric system or Darwin's discovery of the descent of humanity. It was necessary historically for liberal Lutheran theology to arise with intellectual courage to reckon with plausible alternative accounts of nature than that provided by traditional and more literal readings of biblical narrative—even if on examination from this distance, we can now see that traditionally literal readings of the Bible, especially on the creation, have more to do with Aristotle than with Scripture.[4]

Having said that, as important as biblical criticism came to be for the theology of liberal Lutheranism, its significance is more negative than positive. It broke the grip of Orthodoxy but did not in of itself suggest a way forward.

3. Soskice, *Metaphor and Religious Language*.
4. Dillenberger, *Protestant Thought and Natural Science*.

## LUTHERAN THEOLOGY

The scholarly progress of biblical criticism made implausible for thinking people the kind of biblical resourcing practiced in Lutheran Orthodoxy with its rationalistic foundation in the increasingly dubious doctrine of the miraculous dictation of a text without error in any and all respects. It was by no means clear, however, what could take the place of Lutheran Orthodoxy's dogmatic theology epistemologically founded on biblical inerrancy—its polemical alternative to papal infallibility. Indeed nineteenth-century Catholics made a virtue of necessity, arguing that the collapse of biblical authority under the impact of historical criticism gave all the more reason for papal infallibility. Liberal theology took its positive step after biblical criticism by appropriating ethical idealism and it is the viability of this appropriation that constitutes the root theological question we are examining in this chapter on the theology of liberal Lutheranism—a project which in a nontrivial sense may have proved to have been oxymoronic, in so far as theology with Luther would continue to assert a claim to truth in its production of doctrine about the identification of God in and for our troubled world.

For our theological purposes, then, we can begin our study of this chapter in the history of Lutheran theology with modernity's greatest philosopher, the nominal Lutheran Immanuel Kant. Late in life he published a polemical essay, *The Conflict of the Faculties*,[5] in which he codified for the future of European civilization a deeply principled agnosticism with respect to the knowledge of God. He thus banned traditional theological statements from public life which was instead henceforth to be ruled by the "Tribunal of Reason." What we can know is not God, then, but only human representations (graphic, ritual, or conceptual) of God. Traditional dogmatists could believe whatever they wanted in private but

5. See above, 86n82.

## The Idealistic Theology of Liberal Lutheranism

Kant's Tribunal of Reason now policed the public-private boundary and forbade transgression whenever dogmatists interfered in public matters within the claims to know God. On the other hand religious scholars could help with human understanding of how deity is figured, experienced, represented, or conceptualized, since these play a role for good or for ill in human culture.

Here too, however, a reading of Luther could be mustered. Luther too spoke of "two kingdoms," one heavenly and eternal and the other earthly and temporal. After the rise of Pietism (Kant spent part of his youth in a Moravian school), it was not difficult to associate intense inward religious devotion in the experience of conscience with the eternal and heavenly kingdom and to disassociate it from the brutal realities of public life during the rise in Europe of domestic industrialization and the consequent need for raw materials through foreign colonialist adventures. It is important to bear in mind this new set of associations and disassociations of the public-private binary when discussing the role of Luther's "two-kingdoms" theology in the nineteenth century and beyond, inasmuch as for Luther the doctrine meant that God the Creator in overarching conflict with the Satanic usurper battled to regain the afflicted creation for his reign both through the provisional work of temporal authorities and through the everlasting work of spiritual authority. As Luther thought it crucially important to distinguish the temporal regime that God governs by reward and punishment backed by the coercive "power of the sword," from the spiritual regime that God governs through the Word and the Spirit, this two kingdoms theology simply is not modernity's characteristic and highly problematic dualism of public and private spheres.

In Kant's day theories were in the air which purported to explain religion as the mistaken, prescientific account of the awe-full experience of the primitive, prescientific human before the overwhelming powers of indifferent nature. Kant wished both to exploit this theoretical demythologization of tales of the gods as the basis of theological dogmatism and at the same time to elevate a mature and enlightened humanity, courageous enough to think for itself, whose vocation (as Fichte who followed Kant made explicit shortly after Kant's death) was now to play the role to which God or the gods had previously been assigned. Kant named this human experience of anxiety before overwhelming nature "the feeling of the sublime."

Kant analyzed the experience of the sublime as given rise by what appears "contrapurposive for our power of judgment, and as it were violent to our imagination." Consider, he continues, "threatening rocks, thunderclouds piling up in the sky and moving about accompanied by lightning and thunderclaps, volcanoes with all their destructive power, hurricanes with all the devastation they leave behind, the boundless ocean heaved up, the high waterfall of a mighty river, and so on. Compared to the might of any of these, our ability to resist becomes an insignificant trifle."[6] The "sublime" is this experience of chaos interrupting otherwise ordered nature, the "wildest and most ruleless disarray and devastation, provided it displays magnitude and might." Awful and majestic, such natural events are, or at least seem to be the source of the feeling of the sublime. Indeed, as Kant continues on to the theology he wishes to demolish, with "earthquakes, and so on, we usually present God as showing himself in his wrath but also in his sublimity..."[7]

The point of the analysis is that such remnants of primitive superstition divinizing intimidating displays of natural power can be left behind by enlightened minds. But

6 Kant, *Critique of Judgment*, 120.
7 Kant, *Critique of Judgment*, 122.

## The Idealistic Theology of Liberal Lutheranism

the threat to human dignity before strange and awesome nature, a double-headed Shiva giving both order and disorder indifferently to human purposes, remains. Because of the threat to human dignity by the overwhelming powers of nature indifferent to human purposes, Kant could not leave the matter of the sublime behind at this point in his analysis. There are no happy grounds to judge the beautiful in ordered nature as analogous to the work of a beneficent and intentional artist for us to enjoy and imitate, because we cannot at the same time honestly ignore the threatening chaos in nature, analogous to a capricious destroyer. With respect to human dignity, nature is ambiguous—much like Luther's speculative "God hidden in majesty."

Two centuries later we might wonder why this latter face of Nature showing in earthquake and tsunami should not also provide a mediating concept or model for humanity's purposes in relation to itself and nature, as the Nazi summons to re-naturalization,[8] or as the "creative destruction" of fanatical capitalism, would conclude from the same considerations. Although Kant discredited Christian dogma, however, he continued to presuppose the Christian ethic as a cultural commonplace. The categorical imperative of human dignity is to regard other bearers of reason as an end, never as a means, that is, with the same dignity with which one regards oneself as a bearer of reason. This is a de-dogmatized iteration of the Sermon on the Mount's Golden Rule, itself grounded in the dogma of Genesis 1:26–28 that all humans have value as made in the image of God for likeness to God. Culturally, Kant could still presuppose this.

---

8. "Those who want to live, let them fight, and those who do not want to fight in this world of eternal struggle do not deserve to live. Even if this were hard—that is how it is! Assuredly, however, by far the harder fate is that which strikes the man who thinks he can overcome Nature, but in the last analysis only mocks her. Distress, misfortune, and diseases are her answer." Hitler, *Mein Kampf*, 289.

But a mere century after Kant, Nietzsche would understand that from within the immanent limits of nature to create is always also to destroy. Artistic creation within nature can be nothing more than the refashioning of previously existing forms, reduction to material that can be re-utilized by the sovereign self of modernity. And this predation by thinking things extends without remainder upon any and all extended things, including human bodies. If nature capriciously gives and takes, why shouldn't humans do the same just to demonstrate sovereignty?

Sensing the difficulties to come, Kant argued for an interpretation of the sublime as human self-transcendence rather than anything that could be equated with the merely sensual experience of nature's immensity. Just as tales of the gods falsely represent superior forces of nature, the feeling of the sublime is falsely attributed to the experience of this awful majesty. But this is a category mistake, he argued, an anthropomorphism just like the primitive tales of the gods, deifying natural powers like fire, air, or water. Impersonal nature has no 'face.' In fact, the feeling of the sublime elicited by experiences of disorder in nature arises from within; the real source of the feeling of the sublime is the human's own "supersensible power," the "use that judgment makes"[9] of this experience of powerful nature. "We like to call these objects sublime because they raise the soul's fortitude above its usual middle range and allow us to discover in ourselves an ability to resist which is of a quite different kind . . ."[10] This inner ability to resist natural threats to human dignity is more than the tranquil resignation of the Stoic: "though the irresistibility of nature's might makes us, considered as natural beings, recognize our physical impotence, it reveals in us at the same time an ability to judge ourselves independent of

9. Kant, *Critique of Judgment*, 106.
10. Kant, *Critique of Judgment*, 120.

## The Idealistic Theology of Liberal Lutheranism

nature, and reveals in us a superiority over nature that is the basis of a self-preservation quite different from the one that can be assailed and endangered by nature outside us. This keeps the humanity in our person from being degraded . . ." The experience of the sublime is this self-transcending grasp of the supreme dignity of the human being as a bearer of reason; it "is not contained in anything of nature, but only in our mind, insofar as we can become conscious of our superiority to nature within us, and thereby also to nature outside of us . . ."[11] In other words, if we may parody a little, in *knowing* that the avalanche is about to bury me alive, I transcend the crushing load impending my own merely physical annihilation and thus show myself superior in dignity to the purely mechanical fall of tons of accumulated snow tumbling down to crush me under the impersonal sway of the law of gravity.[12] What is sublime is not the avalanche but my knowing comprehension of its lethal might.

This self-transcending perception of the superiority of the thinking human mind over the extended thing of its physical body enmeshed in the causal nexus, occasioned as it is by the experience of natural forces threatening physical existence, licenses the decisive theological move for the era of Lutheran theological liberalism which Kant now makes: the prophetic language of *the wrath of God* is to be stricken from enlightened vocabulary as inimical to rational human self-respect: "the mental attunement that befits the manifestation of such an object is not a feeling of the sublimity of our own nature, but rather submission, prostration, and feeling of our utter impotence . . . worship with bowed head

11. Kant, *Critique of Judgment*, 123.

12. Kant, *Critique of Judgment*, 120–21. The parody is permissible; Kant concedes: "I admit that this principle seems farfetched and the result of some subtle reasoning" (Kant, *Critique of Judgment*, 120–21).

and accompanied by contrite and timorous gestures and voice . . ."[13] Ruling out of rational bounds the prophetic discourse of the wrath of God against the ruin of the creation by human sinners and demonic usurpers, the sublime in nature, history, and eschatology alike is thus domesticated. Language of God henceforth shifts from the telling forth the drama of "sin and grace" to become the progressive rhetoric of "grace overcoming nature" by historical progress (rather than overcoming wrath by the forgiveness of sin).

It cannot be underestimated how profoundly this new "nature-grace" paradigm informed the theology of liberal Lutheranism. The antecedent biblical narrative of creation and fall, redemption and fulfillment was eclipsed by it. The human predicament was now understood as that of "rising beasts" not "fallen angels," building the Kingdom of Ends on the earth;[14] humans are no longer guilty mortals exiled from paradise, at war with God, others, self, and nature too, and thus in need, of a new and true son of David to deliver them. Indifferent Nature, not the holy wrath of the Trinity of love, is the enemy of the human spirit whose self-transcendence was no longer understood as *superbia* (Latin: pride) but as rational self-respect and the basis for the regard of others.

Perhaps the greatest German Lutheran theologian of the nineteenth century was Albrecht Ritschl although his influence was international in scope. Following the pioneering work of the preeminent post-Kantian, Friedrich Schleiermacher (who was in the Reformed tradition), Ritschl engineered the reinvention of Lutheran theology as

13 Kant, *Critique of Judgment*, 122.

14. Kant's programmatic discussion of "The Gradual Transition of Ecclesiastical Faith toward the Exclusive Dominion of Pure Religious Faith in the Coming of the Kingdom of God, in "Religion within the Limits of Mere Reason," in Kant, *Rational Religion*, 146.

## The Idealistic Theology of Liberal Lutheranism

the academic discipline of "systematic" theology at home in the modern university. This reinvention of theology was not a self-evident possibility after Kant's excommunication of dogmatic theology from the field of reason; it came at the cost of redefining theology as knowledge, not of God but of the ideas of God generated by human beings in their experience through history. The purpose of the new academic discipline of systematic theology was to refine and define "the Christian idea of God."

Thus Ritschl wrote programmatically about the new subject matter of reinvented theology: "the religious view of the world, in all its species, rests on the fact that man in some degree distinguishes himself in worth from the phenomena which surround him and from the influences of nature which press in upon him. All religion... conserve[s] and confirms to the personal spirit its claims and its independence over-against the restrictions of nature and the natural effects of human society."[15] Kant was the first, Ritschl acknowledges in the same discussion, "to perceive the supreme importance for ethics of the 'Kingdom of God' [= Kant's 'Kingdom of Ends'] as an association of men bound together by the laws of virtue." The human vocation hence is to build the kingdom of God on the earth. Corresponding to this idealist interpretation of the biblical motif of the kingdom of God, the Christian religion is now to be conceived as "the freedom of the children of God[; it] involves the impulse to conduct from the motive of love, aims at the moral organization of mankind, and grounds blessedness on the relation of Sonship to God, as well as on the Kingdom of God."[16] Thus the sovereign self of modernity is dressed

15. Ritschl, *Christian Doctrine of Justification and Reconciliation*, 17.

16. Ritschl, *Christian Doctrine of Justification and Reconciliation*, 13.

in the garment of biblical rhetoric, the knowledge of God becoming his religious worldview.

Ritschl tells us that such a conception of Christianity is "indispensable for systematic theology," in that the "scientific understanding of the truths of Christianity depends on their correct definition" along these historical and sociological lines. Thus "the first task of systematic theology is correctly and completely to outline and clearly to settle the religious ideas or facts which are included in the conception of Christianity."[17] As the work of sorting, assessing, and systematizing models of the God-human communion in moral purpose on the earth over against the countervailing forces of brute nature, Ritschl utilizes Kantian philosophy as a logical or philosophical space "above Christianity," i.e., "in the general concept of a religious community or fellowship of faith." Thus Ritschl's "systematic" theology is constructive, building on the foundation laid by a general concept of reality. It produces refined and defined ideas of God. Of course, construction is not creation out of nothing but out of something, creatively refashioned for new purposes. Thus the historical critical dimension of constructive theology is to determine the distinctive nature or "essence" of particular religions *as communion with God* or *union with the All*. This is the "something" which systematic theology newly construes. The result of this procedure for Ritschl is that the Christian idea of God now appears as the terminus ad quem of the feeling of the sublime, of self-transcendence, of the dignity of human personality. God guarantees the dignity of the human as a bearer of reason, distinguished from the animal kingdom by virtue of this capacity of intelligent life for self-transcendence.

17. Ritschl, *Christian Doctrine of Justification and Reconciliation*, 14.

## The Idealistic Theology of Liberal Lutheranism

The systematic determination of such theological ideas about God as love, however, can never rest with any particular, historically given materials. History is still in progress! Historically particular conceptions of the divine in any case are now to be treated in the ancillary discipline of the critical history of religions. Systematic theology is to use the fruits of this scholarship further to advance the progressive refinement of the idea of God. Its task, then, is constructive. With just a little tweaking, we can see how the liberal Lutheran theology of the nineteenth century becomes today's "critical theory," the invention of useful ideas of God with an emancipatory intention.

What Ritschl's liberal Lutheran theology did achieve on behalf of much of the modern Christian world was an elevation of the idea of love as marking the supreme representation of God. The notion of God as love in turn made Christianity the evolutionary fulfillment of the history of religions. Surely this was in many respects an achievement when we bear in mind the bloodstained hands of fanatical antecedent orthodoxies, Lutheran and otherwise, of the recent Christian past in Europe. A century later George Lindbeck would capture the achievement of liberal Lutheranism with a little parable, asking whether the Crusader who cries, "Jesus is Lord," as he lops off the head of the infidel, is telling the truth. Lindbeck's implication seems to be that the acclimation, "Jesus is Lord," must be performed in accordance with the act of divine love which the name of Jesus denotes if the statement is to be performatively true. Conversely the statement is falsified when its performance manifestly contradicts the One who came not to be served but to serve and lay down his life a ransom for many. This heightened ethical sensibility of liberal Lutheranism for the use of language about God was its historical achievement and enduring contribution. It can even claim roots in Luther's own concern for how language about God is used, whether to curse or to bless, to promise or demand and so on. Theology today in Luther's tradition will want not to leave this aspect of liberal Lutheranism behind as it moves critically beyond the profound problems of liberal Lutheran theology's foundational dependence on ethical idealism.

David Lotz thus rightly observed in this connection: "It is particularly noteworthy that both Ritschl and [Lutheran] Orthodoxy failed to grasp Luther's profound doctrine of God in which the divine love and wrath were held together in dialectical tension. Ritschl simply dismissed the notion of God's wrath as incompatible with the theological procedure which comprehends God from the perspective of eternity, i.e., in the light of God's Kingdom as the final end of the world, the idea of God's love alone has validity ... Ritschl thus eliminated the idea of God's wrath as a subjective illusion . . ."[18] Yet the prophet Amos had thundered against the loveless indifference of wealthy Israel to impoverished Israel, "Hate what is evil! Love what is good!" And the Apostle Paul echoed Amos centuries later, writing, "let love be sincere; hate what is evil." Biblically, the opposite of God's love is not "hate," but apathy and indifference. Divine love must be against what is against love and that, strictly speaking, is what is meant by the "wrath" of the God of love. As we shall see in the next chapter, both the German Dietrich Bonhoeffer and the Japanese Kazoh Kitamori—as they endured murderous fascist regimes—retrieved Luther's more "dialectical" doctrine of God to critique the false confidence and triumphalist self-understanding of modern Lutheranism representing itself as the evolutionary goal of the history of religions with their Luther no longer a medieval Catholic monk reforming Christendom but an updated reformer and refiner of religion as such.

18. Lotz, *Ritschl and Luther*, 185 n86.

## The Idealistic Theology of Liberal Lutheranism

For the present as we draw this chapter to a close, we note that Kant's root dualism of the phenomenal and the noumenal, sensible and supersensible, associated in turn theologically with the distinction between human and divine as between Spinoza's *natura naturata* (Latin: natured nature) and *natura naturans* (Latin: naturing nature) forbade any identification of God within time and space. Though its import is theologically agnostic, this Kantian dualism lies at the root of the fundamental cognitive claim of liberal Lutheran theology. It is held axiomatically; it is purely negative in content, really a kind of rule or stipulation. *God is inexpressible*; thus any claim to identify the noumenal deity with a phenomenal reality which would declare God is "idolatrous." So much the worse, of course, for the antecedent theological tradition over against which "modern" theology positioned itself. But this puts liberal Lutheran theology in an oxymoronic posture, as if to speak of God knowledgeably when in fact it speaks only of representations of God which in the end prove useful to us. The descent into the Feuerbach trap, as Karl Barth would perceive, becomes inevitable: theology reduces to anthropology. How in any case can this square with Luther's reformatory manifesto, "man wants to be God and does not want God to be God"?

If we can leave behind the false obstacle created by Orthodoxy's doctrine of inerrant Scripture, we can more precisely see that it was the trinitarianism of the antecedent theological tradition which—rightly, properly—offended modern sensibilities with their imperial ambitions. Trinitarianism articulates the fundamental perception in Christianity of the God of love who speaks, is spoken, and is heard, not only in heaven but also on the earth. The trinitarian God is expressible—even if here the human knowledge of God in theology suffers a certain metaphysical deflation: knowledge of God is here a matter of access and identification within contested history rather than theoretical comprehension of the infinite by finite creatures. God declares God in God to us and for us. That being-in-communion is the eternal mystery of God and thus the ground for his saving temporal self-presentation which in turn dares to make the predication of the man born of Mary and executed under Pontius Pilate as "of the same being" as the one whom he addressed, "Abba! Father!" This trinitarianism is intimately connected with Luther's more dialectical doctrine of God in that, as the twentieth-century Lutheran theologian Robert Jenson provocatively put it, in raising the crucified Jesus from death, God decides what kind of God God will be.

Already at the beginning of the nineteenth century a minority report working for a more "dialectical" theology emerged along these trinitarian lines over against the predominance of theological Kantianism. Indeed, Friedrich Hegel in time emerged as the second most prominent Lutheran philosopher of the nineteenth century after Kant. From his early theological education, Hegel understood the vital role trinitarianism had played in the past and took note of this importance in his own revealing critique of it. Consequently, at least some of his followers (the so-called "right wing Hegelians" like Isaiah Dorner) took liberal theology in a more promising direction. But in Hegel, too, the Kantian philosophical space above theology remains enthroned, transcending the "positive" religious representations in human history. From this perspective of the Tribunal of Reason, Hegel could go so far as to acknowledge the truth represented by religious symbols, rituals and concepts, but only to insist that it was philosophy alone that comprehended the truth concealed in religious representations.

## The Idealistic Theology of Liberal Lutheranism

The result of this philosophical captivity is that throughout the nineteenth century we see Lutheran theology, whether inspired more by Kant or by Hegel, turning to historical studies. The great thinkers in Luther's tradition from the time of liberal Lutheranism—ranging from Ferdinand Christian Baur in biblical studies and Theodosius Harnack in Luther studies to his son Adolf Harnack who mastered nineteen centuries of the history of dogma—were historians, not systematicians. But this academic turn from dogma to history under the prevailing assumption of a vaguely theological belief in progress perished in the five-year bloodbath of the Great War. Thinking people of the Enlightenment had asked after the wars of religion, "If this is the religion of the Prince of peace, who needs it?" In another manifestation of the double crisis of modernity, thinking people after the Great War asked, "If this is the denouncement of the religion of progress, who wants it?" The "idea" of God as love died in the trenches.

# 4

# NEO-ORTHODOXY AND THE RENEWAL OF TRINITARIANISM

The appellation "Neo-Orthodox" was disliked by its best early representatives in the "dialectical theology" of the 1920s: the crypto-Lutheran Karl Barth, the radical Lutheran Rudolf Bultmann, and the "religious socialist," Paul Tillich, who later pioneered a path for contemporary neo-liberal Lutheran theology. Barth regularly distanced himself from contemporary Lutherans but in fact his major achievement was to overcome the classical doctrine of Reformed Orthodoxy of double predestination based upon a necessitarian notion of divine simplicity—and he did so on the basis of the classical doctrine of Lutheran Orthodoxy regarding the universality of the atonement. Bultmann explicitly sanctioned his controversial program

## Neo-Orthodoxy and the Renewal of Trinitarianism

for "demythologizing" the New Testament kerygma on a radicalized interpretation of the doctrine of justification, a position shared by Paul Tillich. Tillich, who was a chaplain in the German army during World War I, experienced deeply and painfully the death of the Christian "idea" of God as love and began to articulate a post-Christendom theology of history for discerning revolutionary moments (Greek: *kairos*) turning humanity towards what he later called the "Spiritual Community"—a notion mediating between Christian ecclesiology and eschatology.

With the help of the rediscovery of the post-Hegelian Danish religious thinker Soren Kierkegaard and under the impact of the renegade son of a Lutheran pastor, Friedrich Nietzsche, it was existentialism which gave a new lease on life to theology after the disintegration of the progressive theology of Lutheran liberalism in the trenches of the Great War. To oversimplify, existentialism is the doctrine that brute existence—the surd fact of being thrown into the world and awakening thence to the realization that one is as such hurtling towards the nonexistence of death—such brute "existence" is prior to "essence." There is no prior essence that defines or pre-determines one's existence, giving it structure, boundaries, meaning, and purpose. Rather everyone must in radical individuality make their own personal meaning out of the absurd fact of human existence. One might well wonder in retrospect how existentialism could give Christian theology a new lease on life when it seemed to be predicated on a profound metaphysical nihilism, yet these theologians found it useful for the urgency with which it expressed the burning question of meaningful existence after the mass brutalization of mechanized total war. The radical questioning of the complacent meaning hitherto attributed to humanity by the nineteenth century's faith in progress suggested to these Lutheran theologians that Luther's distinction between God hidden and God revealed could interpret the felt contrast between the experience of metaphysical nihilism and the need for existential meaning.

Yet even these best known figures of early Neo-Orthodoxy still operated under the aegis of Kantian philosophy with its strict and mutual delimitation between the spheres of public and rational thinking and private and religious feeling. Characteristically this dualism came to expression in the strong distinction made in the German language between *Historie* and *Geschichte*. Both words are translated into English by "history," but the first has the connotation of objective factual chronology detailing what really happened as ascertained by critical research while the second has the connotation of narrative, going beyond chronology to stitch facts together into a satisfying story speaking dramatically to the human quest for meaning. These theologians also maintained Kantian reserve towards the unknowable noumenal realm posited to stand behind the phenomenal world of appearances, transposing this into a theology in which God as such remains hidden beyond all human representations by which God is figured in the phenomenal world, though in fact the mature Karl Barth pressed hard against this implication of Kantianism and its contemporaneous Lutheran appropriations.

This same intellectual culture in Germany after the First World War was populated by notable neo-confessionalist Lutheran theologies like those of Paul Althaus and Werner Elert, although their lights have dimmed dramatically in recent times as revelations of their complicity during the rise of Nazism have become better known. Althaus and Elert notoriously signed the "Ansbach Memorandum," claiming to represent "the authentic voice of Lutheranism" over against the anti-Nazi

## Neo-Orthodoxy and the Renewal of Trinitarianism

"Barmen Declaration," which had been authored largely by the Swiss Reformed Karl Barth. The memorandum expressed gratitude for the gift of God, Adolf Hitler, to the German people in their time of need. The complicity of Althaus and Elert stands in striking contrast to the public opposition to Hitlerism by Barth, Bultmann, and Tillich, stances that endangered them personally, with Barth and Tillich fleeing Germany while Bultmann, who remained in Germany, remained at risk throughout the war for his identification with the Confessing Church.

Pride of place in the second generation of Neo-Orthodox Lutheran theology belongs to the younger member and martyr, Dietrich Bonhoeffer, who could have escaped to the United States in 1939 but deliberately and resolutely returned to suffer with his people in hope of being a credible voice for reconstruction after Hitler passed from the scene. Eventually he participated in the military conspiracy to assassinate Hitler—a remarkable turn for a theologian who from youth had considered himself a pacifist after his elder brother had died in World War I. The legacy of Bonhoeffer has been quite contested. Secular and death-of-God theologies in the 1960s claimed him as their predecessor. But upon careful examination in more recent scholarship,[1] Bonhoeffer turns out to have been seriously Lutheran in his theological intention. In what follows we will lift up the abortive "Bethel Confession," which he co-authored with fellow Lutheran Herman Sasse, in the summer of 1933—a full year before the Barmen Declaration. Their draft, however, was sabotaged by theologians sympathetic to Nazism for characteristically modern Lutheran reasons. Their revised version that appeared months later was so compromised that Bonhoeffer disowned it. Yet the suppressed draft of the original Bethel Confession, which biographer Ebehard Bethge preserved

1. DeJonge, *Bonhoeffer's Theological Formation*.

and published, reveals a Bonhoeffer who had deeply internalized Luther's criticism of "enthusiasm," which, as we heard in chapter 2, is Luther's term for the false teaching that the Spirit speaks apart from the external word concerning Christ. As we shall see, Bonhoeffer diagnosed the false theology of the pro-Nazi German Christian party quite precisely in this way as an outbreak of "enthusiasm."

After the defeat of Nazism, the second generation list in Neo-Orthodox Lutheran theology extends to especially prominent theologians like Wolfhart Pannenberg, Eberhard Jüngel, and Robert Jenson. All three of these worked in the modern academic genre of "systematic" theology, which, as noted in the last chapter, went largely missing in nineteenth-century Lutheranism's turn to historical studies. But the tension in genre may run even deeper. We will also attend to the significant Lutheran theologian, Oswald Bayer, who declined to write a "system" of theology on the grounds that it was inimical to the wayfaring stance of Luther's theology of the cross which he sought in his life's work to reactualize as a modern possibility. We will also consider a similar exponent of the theology of the cross in the Japanese Kazoh Kitamori. Kitamori's narrowly focused but sharp critique of Platonizing versions of the christological "two natures" doctrine was executed with an explicit appeal to Luther's more dialectical doctrine of God. This tantalizing move, in tandem with his intentionally non-Western cultural synthesis with indigenous Japanese and Buddhist sources, points forward to the future globalization of Lutheran theology that is now appearing on the contemporary scene. Interestingly Kitamori, like Pannenberg, Jüngel, and Jenson (though not Bayer who published on the "Anti-Kant" gadfly Johann Georg Hamann), was also an exponent of the "right wing" Hegelianism of the nineteenth century. In short if Lutheran theology in the nineteenth century was delimited by Kant's philosophy, in the twentieth century it was much inspired by Hegel's.

In this chapter we will discuss first the generation of Barth, Bultmann, Tillich, and Bonhoeffer whose Lutheran theologies were forged in the crucible of Nazi Germany. Following that we will discuss the second-generation Neo-Orthodox figures, each as a significant marker of the several possible future trajectories of theology in the tradition of Luther, remembering that these arise in the aftermath of Lutheran theology's bitter dalliance with fascism in Germany. Future trajectories are possible. While British and American war propaganda, popularized in William Shirer's influential *The Rise and Fall of the Third Reich*, indulged the trope, "Luther—Bismarck—Hitler," a political order privileging pluralistic freedom of conscience and religious liberty and assigning to secular politics the theologically limited but all the same significant temporal task of human welfare on the good earth can in fact claim Luther as precedent. But this turn towards a global civic future, human rights, and representative secular government was not clear in the period of early Neo-Orthodox Lutheranism when the alternative to fascism for many if not most in Europe was not capitalism-cum-liberal parliamentarianism but Bolshevism.

For all the differences between the University of Berlin rivals, the Reformed Schleiermacher and the Lutheran Hegel, a century later their common inheritance from Kant's "turn to the human subject" appeared to have led to a widespread "domestication of transcendence"—a kind of de facto pantheism in which divine immanence backed the liberal Lutheran theology of human historical progress in building the kingdom of God on earth. This idealistic faith in God as love, making things every day and in every way a little bit better shattered to pieces in World War I. The

Berlin-educated disciple of liberal Lutheran Adolf Harnack and at the time himself a member of the liberal school of theology, Karl Barth, watched in horror as Harnack with all the other prominent representatives of the theological establishment gathered around the Kaiser to affirm Germany's war aims. In search of a fresh start theologically, Barth went back to the Scriptures, particularly to Paul's Epistle to the Romans. This turn was concurrent with the ferment in Luther studies surrounding the publication at long last of the critical edition of Luther's Works (the so-called Weimar edition). Luther's long forgotten theology of the cross was rediscovered and this rediscovery prompted fresh perception of the actual distance between Luther and Lutheran Orthodoxy in the Luther Renaissance mentored by Berlin scholar, Karl Holl.

While the commentary Barth produced on Romans had as much to do with Kierkegaard's nineteenth-century existentialist protest against the essentialist overconfidence which the melancholy Dane saw in the systems of Hegel and Schleiermacher, Barth's Romans asserted forcefully "the infinite qualitative difference" between Creator and creature. This fresh assertion of the christological two-natures doctrine, however, was "dialectical" in the sense that the early Barth saw the unknowable God dynamically touching the earth tangentially at the sole and excruciating point of the cross of Christ and its proclamation—like a bolt out of the blue from above. What remains behind is not dogma to be possessed confidently by the pious or history to be forged by the activist but a crater in the midst of their erstwhile playground.

We are treating Barth as a "crypto-Lutheran" theologian because it is simply impossible to tell the story of Neo-Orthodox Lutheran theology without him. Admittedly, one has to penetrate a great deal of hostile polemic against the ex-liberal, socialist-sympathizing, Swiss Reformed bull who crashed the China shop of establishment Lutheran theology in Germany (on loathsome display, for example, in Lowell Green's defense of his Nazi-sympathizing heroes, Elert and Althaus[2]). We have already mentioned how Althaus and Elert proclaimed themselves over against Barth as the "authentic voice of Lutheranism," thanking God for the gift of Hitler. In any case, one can hardly blame a theologian like Barth, not confessionally Lutheran, for relying on what self-consciously Lutheran scholars and theologians were saying about Luther. One must therefore penetrate past many of the less than complimentary remarks Barth makes about Luther to discern instead a covert rebuke rather to what contemporary Lutherans claim in Luther's name, a polemic that was exacerbated after the war by the fall of the Third Reich. But in point of fact important features of Barth's maturing theology reveal a lifelong engagement with, and a more penetrating appropriation of, Luther's legacy. As we shall see, the most significant German Lutheran theologian at the beginning of the second generation of Lutheran Neo-Orthodoxy was Dietrich Bonhoeffer. His dependence on Barth as a fresh way of appropriating Luther can hardly be denied. We will lift up here several roadblocks to understanding Barth's own engagement with Luther.

Barth was often criticized by Lutheran theologians (and even by fellow Reformed theologians like Emil Brunner) for the preeminence he assigned to the category of "revelation" in his theology and the "objectivity" which he attributed to God's self-revelation in it. They complained that this made intellectual knowledge of God the only difference between the subjectivity of faith and the subjectivity of unfaith—a charge intensified when coupled with anxiety about Barth's supposed "universalism": in the eyes

2. Green, *Lutherans against Hitler*.

of critics it was as if everyone is saved, though not everyone knows it yet. But this is manifestly a misreading of Barth on two different levels. Just like Luther, Barth wants to distinguish God's *self*-revelation in the gospel from the Orthodox overreach extending revelation to cover all things mentioned in Scripture, as if the Bible gave us a revealed science in contrast with scientific science. Barth's accent is on *self*-revelation: we learn through Scripture *who* our Creator and Redeemer is, not *what* the creation is. And just like Luther, Barth intends to follow Paul's language about the apocalypse of Jesus Christ, that is, how divine self-revelation assails and transforms the human subject. In the event of God disclosing who God is through the gospel of the crucified and risen Christ, "God reveals himself as our Lord." As an "I" addressing a "Thou," the human subject is transformed into a theological subject with a new and theological existence.

Barth was also attacked by Lutheran theologians for confusing law and gospel, although there is a confusion within Lutheran theology about this as old as the Formula of Concord's ambiguous article on the so-called "third use" of the law. That controversy questioned whether, after the civil use of God's law to restrain injustice and the spiritual use of it to reveal sin, it remained as a rule still valid over the life of the redeemed. To some self-understood "authentic" Lutherans, this third use implied a re-subordination of God's eschatological gift of justification to life under the law. To others, rejection of the third use implied a rejection of progressive sanctification in the Christian's life. The Formula of Concord did not so much solve this conundrum as split the difference.

The paralyzing confusion within contemporary Lutheran theology which Barth diagnosed in these times was seen in a missiological strategy which held that historically,

## Neo-Orthodoxy and the Renewal of Trinitarianism

socially, and psychologically, the law must be imposed before the gospel can be proclaimed.[3] Especially in debates about the foreign mission field of that time, this precedence of law meant that missionaries had first to civilize primitive peoples (according to the nineteenth century's "white man's burden" project of Europeanizing "savages") before daring to share the easily misunderstood gospel with people unprepared to handle its "freedom." In domestic circles of so-called "inner mission," this meant that revivalist preachers within Christendom had first to terrorize the lapsed with threats of fire and brimstone before sharing a gospel accordingly reduced to the rescue of souls from future hellfire. In more mainstream neo-confessionalist circles, this meant a theological strategy of "mediation," if not a forthrightly apologetic method of correlation, where the danger always looms that the tail of a culture's perceived needs comes to wag the dog of God's agenda, which is the coming of his reign through Jesus Christ by the Holy Spirit.

In all these ways Barth saw the traditional law-gospel sequence deriving from Luther as one requiring a normative order of salvation. He learned, however, from his fellow traveler in the 1920s in the early years of the dialectical theology, Rudolf Bultmann, that the Apostle Paul reasoned differently about the sequence from gospel to ethics: it runs from the indicative of grace sovereignly declaring, "you are a beloved child of God," to a creative imperative, "therefore live as a beloved child of God." The Pauline indicative-imperative order prima facie cannot be squared with a psychologizing law-gospel sequence when the latter is taken as a normative order of salvation.

The fireworks around these shibboleths of Lutheran theology obscured Barth's positive appropriation of Lutheran theology that occurred late in the 1930s. Indeed, the most

3. Flett, *Witness of God*.

significant development in Karl Barth's mature theology was his revolutionary revision of the Reformed doctrine of double predestination, which he came to in writing *Church Dogmatics* II/2. In chapter 1 we mentioned how the Lutheran Formulators had rejected the emerging doctrine of an eternal decree by which God had determined the fate of all creatures, electing some for salvation from the foreordained mass of the damned—a picture they mocked as if portraying a military muster in heaven. Historically, this rejection of double predestination sealed the Lutheran-Reformed divorce. We further saw how this rejection was related to the christological divergence raised by the eucharistic controversies. The emergent Reformed doctrine entailed a definite subordination of Christ the eternal Son as no more than an instrument of the absolute will of God, executing a decree therefore decided before him and apart from him. Despite their objection to Calvinism's logically evident inference to double predestination from shared premises about the absoluteness of God, these early Lutherans also could not think their way out of the conundrum deriving from the metaphysical truism about divine simplicity that both sides formally held. So the Orthodox Lutherans, in their rejection of the thinking that sovereign God wills and executes all things, including the evident withholding of faith from some thus destining them to damnation, threw up their hands and called it a mystery. Yet this Lutheran failure of nerve was punctuated by an emphatic protest that the scope of Christ's atoning work was both universal and objective: God was in Christ reconciling *the world* to himself. When Barth came to his revision of the doctrine of election, he depended on this Orthodox Lutheran affirmation of the universal scope of Christ's saving work and its theologically "objective" status within a more trinitarian understanding of God's deity. Bonhoeffer's reading of it is captured in the opening chapter

## Neo-Orthodoxy and the Renewal of Trinitarianism

of his posthumous *Ethics*, "God's Love for the World." Whatever peripheral skirmishes against traditional Lutheran certitudes Barth engaged in, on the central matter of his own theological achievement he may fairly be said to be exposed in this way as a crypto-Lutheran theologian.

A rather more important skirmish occurred with erstwhile comrade in arms from the early days of dialectical theology, Rudolf Bultmann. Bultmann personified a posture which today has lamentably almost disappeared from the scene—a New Testament scholar who is also a theologian. Moreover, he called his most important and controversial program in theology of demythologizing the New Testament for contemporary proclamation nothing but a "radicalization" of the Lutheran doctrine of justification (a position taken up and advanced in the United States by Gerhard Forde under the motto "radical Lutheranism"). As a New Testament scholar, Bultmann realized that the theology of the Apostle Paul was thoroughly stamped by the apocalyptic mythology of Second Temple Judaism. All the basic concepts of Paul, when they are not influenced by Hellenistic mythologies, are stamped by a myth that tells how Satan and his minions of darkness have usurped the groaning earth through their instruments, the powers of sin and death. But to his remnant righteous faithful, the Creator God reveals this predicament and also his plan to end the demonic rebellion and bring about his manifest reign on the earth. For Paul this event of revelation occurred when God exposed his own rebellion, hiding under the guise of Torah piety, by revealing the crucified Jesus, whom he had despised as a lawless blasphemer justly rejected and executed, as instead his saving Lord. This revelation was thus a *crisis* (the Greek word means judgment) in his life which required of him a decision for a new self-understanding.

Now he had to give up all of his old props and securities to risk new life on the basis of a pure gift.

We thus can see already how Bultmann was led by these historical considerations to the existentialist interpretation of myth. He saw his own position prefigured in the Gospel of John, which represented in his eyes a relentless deliteralization of the apocalyptic myth with its literal expectation of Christ's future return in glory, for the sake of present proclamation pressing for the decision of faith to abandon all carnal securities. For Bultmann, myths were something like Hegel's view of religious representations: they concealed a kernel of truth about human existence that is obscured by its husk, that is, if we take the myths literally as telling some tale of the gods. In the process myth is dangerous because literally it "objectifies" the ineffable God by representing God as a worldly figure alongside other figures in the world. When this husk of literal representation is peeled away, however, we discover beneath it the kernel of truth it tells about human existence (the kernel-husk metaphor is one that Luther himself had used and was appropriated in the Kantian theology of the nineteenth century). But the truth discovered is not Hegel's philosophical comprehension of God in humanity's coming to the state of absolute consciousness of its unity with God; rather it is human existential self-understanding in its precarious need, as Kierkegaard would have put it, of making an infinitely passionate decision about one's human existence in a state of objective uncertainty.

There can be little doubt that Bultmann, and many who followed him especially in the postwar Germany of the 1950s, were actually relieved in this way to be delivered by the program of demythologization from the burden of traditional Christian belief, which had already been felt to be a burden, alongside of the Jewishness of Jesus. As

Doris Bergen and Richard Steigmann-Gall have shown us in detailed studies,[4] the German Christians were as anti-doctrinal as they were pro-Nazi, and when they survived scrutiny after the war they continued their contempt of the knowledge of God articulated in Christian doctrine by invoking Bultmann's deliverance from the perceived burdens of creedal belief. Bultmann, to be sure, was far more sophisticated than the clumsy, crude manipulation of Scripture, rejection of the ecumenical creeds, and revision of liturgy undertaken by the German Christians in support of the now discredited Nazism. It came to many as genuine relief: one no longer had to hold the Apostle Paul's manifestly mistaken belief about the second coming of Christ in glory, if radically instead "now is the day of salvation." One could thus be a Christian and a true proclaimer of the gospel when one peeled these outer husks of myth away to offer contemporaries the existential kernel contained within of a new self-understanding. When Bultmann was criticized for this apparently wholesale rejection of traditional Christian belief as myth in need of existentialist reinterpretation, he went on the offensive. Appealing to Luther's "faith alone," he argued that demythologizing was nothing but the radical fulfillment of faith that receives all things as gracious gift without support from objective evidence, objective revelation, or anything else but the word alone announcing divine grace. Indeed, for theologians to offer any extraneous support for the offered gift only compromised the sheer graciousness of the gift. Seeking proof or even evidence for faith is thus a sign of bad faith.

Barth and Bultmann engaged one another in what the German language felicitously calls an *Auseinandersetzung*—setting out their opposing positions in an effort to clarify difference and achieve disagreement. It is important

4. Bergen, *Twisted Cross*; Steigmann-Gall, *Holy Reich*.

to understand here that Barth as well as Bultmann realized that New Testament myth cannot rightly be taken as a literal representation of what actually happened or happens in time and space. Centrally the scholarly rediscovery of New Testament apocalyptic in the twentieth century is not taken as literal predictive prophecy about the end of time but about the time of the end breaking into the fixed oppressions and deceptions of the present age. For Bultmann, this deliteralization is true for two reasons. First, the nature of our sources in the New Testament literature is such that any confident reconstruction of what actually happened in the event of Jesus of Nazareth according to the canons of modern scholarly historiography is not possible. The historical man Jesus is so thoroughly overlaid with post-Easter belief in him expressed in mythological language of apocalyptic that any reconstruction of an historical Jesus is impossible. Thus Bultmann rejected the nineteenth-century liberal quest for the historical Jesus, as disabled by the nature of our sources. This meant for him that modern Christian faith could not be founded on a new, critically ascertained perception of the human consciousness of Jesus. But further, not only could such a foundation not be dug but also careful study of the New Testament material showed that it was only by the gift of Easter faith by means of the word alone that the scandal of the cross is overcome. The report at the empty tomb, "He is not here," catalyzes the statement of faith, "He is risen." Second, Bultmann held to the eminently Kantian objection that mythological language "objectified" the inexpressible God who could only be spoken of in poetry that does not take itself literally. That is to say that Bultmann's theology cannot provide knowledge of God but only indirectly indicate the mystery of grace. Thus grace becomes the abstract figure of God in the world. Of course one wonders then how the figure of grace avoids the fate of reification and thus becoming just another idol alongside other idols, even if it is a "radically Lutheran" idol. Indeed one wonders how the notion of "grace" now performs in decaying Lutheranism in Europe and America. Has "grace" become a cliché? For preaching that "God is not a problem," that there is no need for the "justification" in "justification by faith alone"?

Barth's reasoning was somewhat different, although he agreed with Bultmann about the failure of the liberal quest for the historical Jesus. Barth held that the genuine miracle of God's self-revelation is that God, who always remains subject, nevertheless makes himself object for human knowledge in faith by the event of Jesus Christ. One might say, therefore, that not the abstract notion of "grace," reified into an idol, but rather Jesus Christ crucified and risen is the figure of God in the world. Consequently New Testament mythology is not to be reduced to its supposedly existential kernel but rather interpreted as knowledge of God. Barth expresses this by saying that subject and predicate terms are not convertible: it is God known in Christ who is gracious; grace is not God.

Historically the outcome of this *Auseinandersetzung* between Barth and Bultmann was indecisive. To followers of Bultmann it seemed that Barth was reviving all the problems of premodern dogmatic theology, making historical claims unconscionable for modern people—thus the pejorative term "Neo-Orthodoxy." It seemed to many followers of Barth that Bultmann was, just as Calvinists have always suspected about Lutherans, a monophysite docetist whose Jesus Christ only seemed to be truly human as a real individual amid all the other human individuals of the world. Bultmann's "Jesus" in his "Jesus Christ" was without any historically particular content, nothing but a presupposition and occasion for an unworldly word calling individuals to authentic existence of life without securities.

A side note here is fitting on the so-called New Perspective on Paul, which is largely a sharp reaction in scholarship against the dominant position Bultmann held in New Testament studies through the end of the twentieth century. When proponents tell of their new perspective as one overcoming the "Lutheran" reading of Paul, readers would be well advised to gloss the word "Lutheran" here with the "Bultmannian radical-Lutheran" reading of Paul. The new perspective makes two fundamental criticisms of Bultmann's theology: First, that it presupposes and projects onto Paul the "introspective conscience of the West." This projection finds an existentialist concern for human authenticity in Paul that is not really there, in that Paul is far more interested in the social inclusion of Gentiles in the covenanted people of God than in their states of existential interiority. But the "introspective conscience" of Bultmann's Western cultural tradition inherited especially from Augustine and Luther necessarily focuses everything on the question of the individual's deliverance. This produces a distorted reading of Paul, whose social concern should predominate. Second, the program of demythologizing apocalyptic overlooks the social concern of biblical salvation history, as if God were a Gnostic concerned only with the evacuation of a handful of spiritually elite from a world to be left behind for the devil. Whether either of these problems can actually be found in the historical Luther's reading of Paul is a question that may fairly be put back to the New Perspective.

In any case, an alternative to the positions both of Bultmann and the New Perspective was already enunciated by Bultmann's renegade disciple, Ernst Käsemann. Käsemann resisted the manifest docetic tendencies of Bultmann's Christology by inaugurating the so-called "second quest" for the historical Jesus, which was decidedly not a search for Jesus's inner consciousness or personality, but rather for what can be known historically about his relationship to the one he regarded as God. The modest result of this quest was that historically one can affirm that in his "claim to authority" Jesus's own relation to God betrays an "implicit Christology." Correspondingly also in his Paul interpretation, Käsemann retrieved apocalyptic mythology as "the mother of Christian theology," which cannot be husked off and discarded without denuding the God of the gospel of his saving relation to the usurped world on which the cross of Jesus stood. Despite such penetrating criticisms of Bultmann, Käsemann continued to identify himself as a member of his school in the specific sense of upholding the centrality of Paul's doctrine of justification. This came, however, with a new accent. Käsemann lifted up Paul's precise statement about the justification of the "ungodly" to make it utterly plain that justification is not based on a modern piety of achieved or aspired human authenticity to be gained by a decision of faith, but on the resurrection-asserted Lordship of him who had been crucified, numbered thusly among the ungodly.

The other prominent representative of first-generation Neo-Orthodox Lutheran theology is also the most difficult to classify, Paul Tillich, who actually ended his career as the forerunner of contemporary neoliberal Lutheran theology. Tillich was the pious son of a Lutheran pastor who went patriotically to serve the Kaiser in World War I as a military chaplain. There his acculturated liberal Lutheran Christianity was, in a metaphor he famously used, shaken to the foundations. In the 1920s he virtually laicized, making his living as a philosopher of religion; he joined the first wave of the sexual revolution (according to the sometimes salacious memoir of his long-suffering wife, Hannah), and became active in the ranks of the religious socialists. He was impressed with the prophetic power of Barth's commentary on Romans and followed the movement of dialectical theology until it came to pieces with the rise of Hitlerism. His specific take on Luther was mediated by the nineteenth-century philosopher Friedrich Schelling who had developed Luther's distinction between God hidden and God revealed into a view of God as abysmal depth as well as creative ground of being.

Yet Tillich's early work reflected the contemporaneous rediscovery of biblical eschatology: he wrote of the *kairos*, a Greek word indicating the fullness of time, the time that Bultmann named the eschatological "crisis." Tillich took this prophetic interpretation of time when it becomes ripe for God's revolution as a victory of the universal God of time over the local gods of space. In this vein he wrote an impressive interpretation of Nazism as a resurgence of the tribal deities of space, revolting against the eschatological-universal claim of the Christian message portending the fullness of time in the coming of God's kingdom. Before this book could be published, however, Tillich fled Nazi Germany for Union Theological Seminary in New York where he spent the next thirty years. There he became an American theologian, even returning to the pulpit. Throughout his life Tillich continued to describe himself as a "Lutheran theologian," though his view of justification as being grasped by the new being in Christ has to be classified as something closer to Osiander's notion of the infusion of righteousness than to the mature Luther's view of its attribution by faith by way of the joyful exchange. Yet more than a memory of "forensic" or attributed righteousness is pointedly present in one of his most fondly remembered sermons that psychologically paraphrased the doctrine of justification as the indicative of grace to "accept the fact that you are accepted."

By the end of his American career, however, Tillich was explicitly criticizing Barth's "Neo-Orthodoxy" as a retreat to precritical dogmatism and advancing his own theology in contrast as continuing the great work of liberal Protestant theology that had begun in Schleiermacher. His systematic theology, accordingly, executed a systematic apologetics by means of a "method of correlation." By this he meant that contemporary culture in the form of its philosophical interpretations of human existence asks the questions which theology seeks to answer with the revelation of God in a particular time and place. This was a reprise of Ritschl's mainstream, nineteenth-century German Lutheran theology of "mediation," which interpreted culture as the hidden work of the Creator God. Thus cultural questions could be explicated and thematized as preparation for the gospel, consciously or unconsciously waiting for the revelation of God offered in the Christian message.

Tillich's method produced much, alternately inspiring and provocative, that seemed utterly novel to the ears of his American audience, including statements that seemed to deny that God "exists," or, on the other hand, that Christ would exist even if Jesus never had, or that God is not a "person" but "being-itself." In all this provocation, however, Tillich maintained that he was above all concerned to protect the godliness of God from profanation. His "method of correlation" insisted that theology take into deep consideration the cultural context in which it did its work, foreshadowing the concerns for relevance in contemporary neoliberal theology. His method, along with his innovative language, likewise prepared the ground for the constructivism of contemporary neoliberal theology. Much of liberal Lutheranism in the United States remains in Tillich's debt. His erudition, philosophical breath, and existential preaching lent to American liberal Protestantism an aura of intellectual depth and respectability (although the dominant philosophy of midcentury America under the sway of so-called logical positivism regarded Tillich's synthesis of Greek ontology and biblical drama as "bombast"). For many, Tillich's work opened up for the first time a better understanding of Luther himself than found in the Pietist, confessionalist, or orthodox communities of immigrant American Lutherans.

Our treatment of Dietrich Bonhoeffer requires some background information from Luther's time. In controversies with Andreas Karlstadt and Thomas Müntzer in the earlier years of the Reformation, Luther had developed a powerful critique of what he called in German, *Schwaermerei*. English readers will recognize a common root in their word for a wave of angry buzzing bees, a *swarm*. This colorful metaphor was employed by Luther to characterize self-proclaimed prophets and their demagogic agitprop. As Luther saw it, such prophets typically claimed for their anti-intellectual and populist preaching the authority of the immediate inspiration of the Holy Spirit, disregarding the critical counsel of 1 John 4:1–4 to test the spirits to see whether they are of God. According to that text in 1 John, the criterion for such testing is the coming of Jesus Christ *in the flesh*—as a particular body delimited from other bodies and thus always as external to any other. Luther interpreted this criterion for testing spirits as requiring the "external word" (Latin: *verbum externum*) that comes to the self from outside of the self to tell of Jesus Christ as an historical event for the purpose of transforming the existing self.

Accordingly, as Jesus is the Spirit-anointed Christ, the beloved Son on whom the Father's Spirit dwells, he is the exclusive medium of the Holy Spirit's bestowal for others.

One knows that it is the Holy Spirit just because it is known definitively as the Spirit of the Father and the Son. Thus in Luther's shorthand, the Spirit is given by way of the external word even as the external word is grasped in faith by the Spirit who gives himself to the auditor that she may believe. The circle here is not vicious but hermeneutical and it reflects the trinitarian perception of God: Jesus cannot be the Son that he is apart from the Father's Spirit nor can the Spirit be the Holy Spirit except as the Spirit of the Father of this Son. Perception of this underlying trinitarian knowledge of God may be obscured by the polemical fireworks of Luther's critique of Karlstadt and Müntzer, which was personal for him and thus particularly intense. Karlstadt had been Luther's faculty colleague and co-reformer in Wittenberg while Müntzer was a former student whom Luther had recommended for his first pastoral position. In addition to the personal bitterness, there were high stakes involved in their agitation for the revolutionary destruction of the existing religious and civil forms instead of Luther's mere reformation.

Luther's case against "enthusiasm," along with its tacit trinitarianism worked out in this controversy, became an important ancillary to Luther's theology of the cross. As such Bonhoeffer found in it the decisive precedent for his early critique of the pro-Nazi German Christian party. This word, "enthusiasm," as we learned in the preceding chapter, derives from the Greek and denotes someone who claims to be chock-full of the Spirit. But the spirits must be tested! The *Holy* Spirit is the Spirit of Jesus and his Father, who calls through the gospel and thus is given with the effective calling realized in repentance and faith conforming an existing self to the cross and resurrection of Christ. One who would invoke the Spirit as an authority for preaching God's word apart from this essential reference to Christ and him crucified is an enthusiast who will lead people astray. So, in Luther's judgment, the iconoclast Karlstadt and the insurrectionist Müntzer were doing. In an enormous irony of European history, as mentioned in the last chapter, Luther's neologism, "enthusiasm," was taken up several centuries later by Immanuel Kant and deployed to rule out of rational bounds also the gospel's claim to truth in revealing Jesus as the Christ, the Son of God. But this outlawing of the external word leaves theology blind and incapacitated, incapable of discernment and judgment, uncritically open to any new wind of doctrine just as happened in the rise of pro-Nazi German Christianity.

With this background in mind, we may now turn to Bonhoeffer's Neo-Orthodox doctrine of Scripture and the corresponding conception of theology as witness or confession or, as I prefer to name it, "critical dogmatics." That doctrine makes Scripture and its theological interpretation into a dynamic unity and ongoing task for present witness. This conception stands in significant contrast to the task assigned to exegesis in the old orthodoxy, which amounted to the artificial harmonization of apparent factual contradictions coupled with a conservative apologetic attempt to demonstrate the truth of the Bible as understood by Orthodox Lutheranism. This inward looking orientation of exegesis reflected the situation of competing orthodoxies of the time in the alternately defensive and aggressive postures each held toward its rivals. But the final collapse of such contention for the mantle of Christendom occurred in the bloodbath of the Great War. The aftermath of that catastrophe not accidentally witnessed the rise of the ecumenical movement with which Bonhoeffer identified. Thus the horizon of theological exegesis shifts considerably. The details of Bonhoeffer's innovative doctrine and use of Scripture may be retrieved from a particularly salient but still little-known work, his co-authored 1933 Bethel Confession,[5] which we will now examine in some detail since it charts the future course of Neo-Orthodox Lutheranism.

The canonical Scriptures of the Old and New Testament are said to be the "sole source and measure of the doctrine of the church," yet not, as in Lutheran Orthodoxy, because they are miraculously given as an inerrant text to serve as an epistemological foundation according to the rationalist canons of early modernism. Notably, their theological authority for the Christian community is grounded in their unique historical role as human "witness" to the revelation of God, Jesus Christ, the Person who is the divine Word-made-flesh, crucified and risen from the dead and thus present to faith as this undivided person. "Witness" to Christ is taken as the Spirit-wrought act of "confession" as that is made upon the witness stand in the situation of trial. Thus "witness" is not conceived here as a pious work of religious self-disclosure for the purpose of converting others to the same experience. Witness is instead conceived apocalyptically. From the Hebrew prophets we learn that the Lord has a controversy with his people whom he puts on trial. In this trial God either judges or justifies. The justified in turn justify God in his just judgment—vindicating the justice or righteousness of Jesus Christ for his loving solidarity with sinners incapable of justly justifying themselves. This confession of or witness to the saving righteousness of God in Jesus Christ is the product of properly theological interpretation of Scripture. "In bearing *witness* to these acts of God,

5. The reference is to the August redrafting of an initial outline by Bonhoeffer and Sasse, which for convenience we will simply call "the Bethel Confession." The two versions are printed side-by-side in English translation in Bonhoeffer, *Dietrich Bonhoeffer: Berlin: 1932–1933*, 374–424, and all quotations of the Bethel Confession are taken from this edition. For more detailed treatment from which the present discussion is drawn, see Hinlicky, "Verbum Externum," 189–215.

the Scriptures are God's word to us. The church can only proclaim God's revelation by interpreting this word, which bears *witness* to it" (emphasis added).

This formulation of the authority of the Bible is qualified by the stipulation that it bears this authority when it is rightly interpreted theologically. The Bible has authority because it is the unique human attestation of the divine Word of God the eternal Son made flesh in Christ and in so doing it becomes the present word of God for auditors today when and where the Spirit is pleased to grant faith through its rightly interpreted proclamation. Bonhoeffer here is indebted to Karl Barth but also to his co-author, and the Prussian Union liberal turned Lutheran, Hermann Sasse, who, in accord with Augsburg Confession's Fifth Article on the preaching ministry of the church, taught that the word of God comes as event subject to the sovereignty of the Holy Spirit. This relative subordination of the written word of God to the event of the word of God in preaching or confession is necessary because both biblical and contemporary witness is and remains a human word spoken in history whether by prophets or apostles, preachers or theologians, just as Jesus Christ is and remains human in the event of the incarnation and its subsequent proclamation. To err is human and this applies to the entire history of sacred witness. Interpretation does not blindly affirm whatever the Bible says as if the word of God; rather it probes this unique and indispensable witness of prophets and apostles to uncover the reason good enough for Jesus Christ as God's good news for the lost and perishing creation. Contemporary witness requires ever intelligent *interpretation* of the biblical witness in order to discern the *right* and *timely* word of God against the anti-divine powers and for the sake of penitents *in the present situation of trial*. As an act of faith within history, the act of confession involves contemporaries in the reception,

## Neo-Orthodoxy and the Renewal of Trinitarianism

understanding and articulation of the biblical witness which it appropriates. The witness of faith is always *mediated by prayerful and thus conscientious interpretation* in a concrete situation for a specific audience; the interpretive work of theology, thus taken not as precritical dogmatic *obiter dicta* but as postliberal critical dogmatics, is organic to the intelligent appropriation of Scripture for the purpose of contemporary confession. The proclamation of God's Word as witnessed biblically and at the same time its interpretation theologically for the sake of contemporary proclamation and confession form a dynamic whole.

This quiet shift away from the inerrancy doctrine of Orthodoxy to biblical witness and confessing theology has profound implications in retracing backward the evolution from confession to orthodoxy that occurred historically, as we reviewed in chapter 2. There it was underscored how the ecumenical intention of the Augsburg Confession was eclipsed by its retooling as the charter legal document of a rival orthodoxy among others. Precisely as Bonhoeffer was engaged in the postwar ecumenical movement and willing, as a Lutheran, to learn from the Reformed theology of Barth (and Barth likewise, as shown above, from Lutheran theology), he came to this fresh understanding of scriptural authority. The Bible is not put forward now as some miraculous alternative to science and philosophy, calling on the faithful to deny the Big Bang or the Descent of Species; rather the crucified and risen Christ is understood, proclaimed, and confessed as the present and saving Lord in whom the controversy of God with the fallen creation is prosecuted in order that it be reconciled. In a fresh and disturbing way, therefore, this controversial Christ of the Scriptures becomes the hermeneutical key to understanding the "one time, unrepeatable and self-contained history of salvation" of the Genesis-to-Revelation biblical canon. Conversely, Christ can be known this way, as reconciliation with God who is in controversy with his wayward creation, only when the Bible is taken as a canonical whole, since indispensably it is from the Hebrew prophets that we learn that God's revelation is to be conceived apocalyptically as controversial: a trial, a contention with the world for the sake of the world, even also against the church for the sake of the church.

God's Word is thus both prophetic critique and apostolic reconciliation; it is both of these distinct words, yet never one without the other, a living, dynamic whole pressing into the here-and-now in the figure of the crucified and risen Christ, who is confessed or denied in the crisis of the world thus generated. Contemporary interpretation, therefore, recognizably continues the prophetic controversy of God with the world for the sake of the reconciliation of the world in Christ as the apostolic good news. The proper distinction of law and gospel in God's word is treated in this way, not as an abstract Procrustean bed into which academic theologians force each and every passage of Scripture, thus doing violence to the diversity of scriptural genres. Rather the proper distinction is a hermeneutical one about how Scripture is to be used for contemporary proclamation and confession: whether to accuse, to indict, and to convict or to console, to pardon, and to repair to the end that the afflicted are comforted and the comfortable are afflicted.

Not surprisingly, then, there is no paragraph in the Bethel Confession devoted to the shibboleth of modern Lutheran theology, a dualistic antagonism between particularist Jewish legalism and inclusive Christian love. In the Bethel Confession's contemporary context, prominent liberal Lutherans like Bonhoeffer's teacher, Harnack, had in the recent past championed the second-century semi-Gnostic heretic Marcion and advocated the excision of Old Testament Scripture from the Christian canon. Under the aegis of unfurled swastikas the German Christians were taking up Harnack's banner, demanding de-Judaization of the Bible. Bonhoeffer and Sasse, tacitly responding to this, not only take "law" as the holy God in the office of Judge rather than as "Jewish legalism," but they also coordinate divine law and gospel with Luther's purpose clause: God wounds *in order* to heal, God afflicts *in order* to comfort, God kills *in order* to make alive. That coordination of divine law and gospel accords with the argumentative burden in the Bethel Confession to lift up the law of Israel, the Ten Commandments, as God's own law in distinction from the positive law of the nations, or the so-called "orders of creation" or even the natural law of Roman Catholic social teaching, let alone the self-righteous legalism polemically attributed to Judaism. Likewise, while the Bethel Confession's article on Justification and Faith affirms the central Lutheran conviction that "faith clings solely to the biblical word of the promise of God's grace," it immediately and pointedly protests against "the confusion of trust in God with faith."

This last statement may cause bewilderment today. It requires further elaboration in that it makes a frontal assault on another shibboleth of existentialist Lutheranism, which tries to downplay intellectual belief by exalting blind but heartfelt trust as the humanly authentic stance elicited by the liberating word. Given the historical criticism of Bible and of dogma, followed by the widespread modern-Lutheran reduction of faith from knowledge of God to contentless albeit sincere trust or existential authenticity, the Bethel Confession's protest here is highly instructive. It sees "heathen fatalism" in heroic Fascist will-power leading directly to blind, self-sacrificing trust in *der Führer*. It contrast to such blind trust the Bethel Confession takes up the critically discerned eschatological belief "that at the end of all things God will create a new heaven and a new earth," that indeed it is "our earth that will be made new, the same earth on which the cross of Christ stood." A vague, contentless *fiducia* (trust) which can be readily enlisted to Fascist struggle, duty, and sacrifice is thus sharply contrasted with Christian faith as an eschatological dogma, spelled out in the final article of the Bethel Confession on the "end of all things."

Given this eschatological belief, the insistent emphasis of the Bethel Confession is on Christ as the unity of the Testaments in the wholeness of Scripture. This unity of New Testament with Hebrew Scriptures has an indispensable function. It assures that the New Testament message is understood as answering not any old question of the zeitgeist but the prophetic question framed by the Old Testament. The gospel is God's answer to God's own question about his rebellious creation. Thus the Gospel is not captured and remade into the instrument of some other framework, as the pro-Nazi German Christians wanted, who were forthrightly demanding the "coordination" of the Christian message with the National Socialist worldview—precisely by way of decoupling Christ from the prophetic legacy of Judaism and thus turning Christ into their Aryan Jew fighter answering to their perceived needs for German liberation. Against this separation, the Bethel Confession insists on the unity of Scripture to ensure that "we are not the judge of God's word in the Bible; instead, the Bible is given to us so that we may submit to Christ's judgment" in the prophetic critique. In its penultimate article on "The Church and the Jews," the Bethel Confession concretely aims at just such an act of obedient *martyria* (witness) at the present hour: "The Christians who are of Gentile descent must be prepared to expose themselves to persecution before they are ready to betray in even a single case, voluntarily or under compulsion, the church's fellowship with Jewish Christians that is instituted in word and sacrament." While in retrospect this demand may seem short-sightedly ecclesiocentric, in August 1933 it was the timely word to and for the church bewitched by the spectacular rise of Hitler.

As mentioned, the Bethel Confession was composed just months after Hitler came to power and almost a full year before the Barmen Declaration. We must avoid the retrospective fallacy in appreciating its contribution. After the fact of the massive Nazi crime in the Final Solution's systematic murder of millions of Jews and others that commenced with the invasion of the Soviet Union in June 1941, it is often lamented that the church cared only for its own, as in the Bethel Confession's just cited commitment to Jewish Christians, thus apparently leaving non-Christian Jews to the nonexistent mercy of the Nazis. Bonhoeffer himself in time lamented this increasingly untimely ecclesiocentric self-concern as Nazism increasingly showed its true face, and thus came to regard it as a failure of the Confessing Church.

Clarity, then, is required here. After the end of Christendom, itself attested by the rise of Nazism in Germany and the endemic possibility of fascism in modern cultures, the Bible has no authority beyond the church—and at that it only exercises any actual authority in the church that intends orthodoxy. Moreover, this Neo-Orthodox conception of biblical witness and contemporary confession also forbids sweeping and uncritically dogmatic pronouncements pretending to a timeless formulation of timeless truth. It critically limits authentic proclamation of the word of God to the present situation such that theology must be continually engaged as the situation changes—always reforming means always reformulating the confession. The Bethel Confession's concrete word of solidarity with Jewish Christians at the time of its composition in 1933 was thus apt just because it was delimited and concrete. The failure lies not in the Bethel Confession, but in its subversion and the consequent failure to persist in the very engagement it would have enacted and modeled.

In any event, contemporary judgment is the goal of confession, and such judgment is binding because "the Holy Spirit that speaks to us through a word in the Holy Scriptures is always the spirit of the whole of Holy Scriptures and thus can never be confused with one's own pious experience in selecting whatever one pleases"—or deselecting whatever one pleases, such as, for example, in the de-Judaizing of the Bible and the church's ministry demanded by the German Christians. Luther's principle *was Christum treibet* (what necessitates Christ) "does not give us room to arbitrarily choose whatever we want from the Scriptures." On the contrary, for Luther it is precisely the prophetic word of the Old Testament which necessitates the crucified Messiah as the reconciliation of the world fallen under the holy judgment of God's law. Thus Luther's famous Christocentric hermeneutical principle tells how we are to receive the *whole* of the Scriptures: "the essence of the Reformation is consciousness of the Holy Scriptures, submission to the Holy Scriptures. For the Reformation, Martin Luther is the teacher who is obedient to the Holy Scriptures."

This nuanced articulation of scriptural authority over against enthusiasm is articulated in a variety of ways in the Bethel Confession that cumulatively validate the claim that its case retrieves Luther's teaching: "God's Word for me is always a foreign one." On Reformation: Luther "fought against blind overestimation of human reason and rejected as a temptation of the devil the human delusion that one could come to God through one's own spirit, without the divine Word." On the Trinity: "We reject any attempt to dismember the revelation of the Trinitarian God, to claim to understand the creation or reconciliation or redemption as a concept on its own." On Creation: "Pious natural knowledge is not capable of comprehending God as Creator and the world as creation . . . We reject the false doctrine that in a particular 'hour of history' God is speaking to us directly and is revealed in direct action in the created world, for it is enthusiasm to think one understands the will of God without the express words of Holy Scripture, to which God is bound." On the orders of creation: "These orders of preservation are therefore of no value in themselves, but only in relation to the end to which God will bring humankind, to the new creation in Christ . . . They are to be distinguished from the law of God. In the law, God speaks through revelation to each human being personally. It represents God's claim to be Lord . . ." On Christ: "The cross of Jesus Christ is not at all a symbol for anything; it is rather the unique revelatory act of God, in which the fulfillment of the law, the judgment of death on all flesh, and the reconciliation of the world with God are carried through for all people." On the Holy Spirit: "the Spirit is given to humankind only through the external Word and the sacraments of the church . . . We reject the false doctrine that the Holy Spirit can be recognized without Christ in creation and its orders . . . The rebellion against this teaching about the Holy Spirit is an ethno-nationalist [*völkisch*] rebellion against the church of Jesus Christ." On the Church: "Thus the church is constituted not by human beings, not even by the faith or the moral qualities of persons, but only by Jesus Christ the Lord: *ubi Christus, ibi ecclesia*." On the Ministry: "The preaching ministry is service to the Word of reconciliation and is therefore the opposite of any magical powers of leadership." On the Nations: "The message of the gospel is equally accessible, or equally inaccessible, to all peoples. For it is only God's Holy Spirit who can bring about faith . . .

The boundaries of the Volk and church are never the same." On the State: "Thus all worldly government, whether good or bad, stands not within the realm of salvation but rather within the realm of death."

Thus we see that according to the Bethel Confession the Reformation's *verbum externum* was not simply a matter of the Bible's formal authority over against private interpretation or of learned hermeneutics over against amateurish reader-response speculation. What is biblical is the coming of its central figure, Christ by the power of the Spirit, a figure drawn from the whole Scripture and uniting in himself God's judgment and justification of his rebellious human creature by way of Christ's own cross and resurrection. Christ comes from outside the self to unite with the self and so to transform the self with *this* judgment and justification which he *is*. The authority of Scripture as the historically unique witness to Christ is recognized and put into effect in the act of interpreting biblical texts *with* this christological key *to* this transformative end. That cannot but be controversial, first of all, within the life of the wayward churches themselves. Thus, critical theology in the tradition of Luther tests the spirits by the *verbum externum*—just such *disputation* is what the Bethel Confession consciously retrieves and presently undertakes. To undertake such disputation, to test the contemporary spirits, to present Christian dogma critically the Bethel Confession had announced its principled method as the dialectic of Spirit and Word from the outset: "Only through the Holy Spirit do we hear the word of God from the Bible. But this Spirit itself comes to us only through the word of the Scriptures in their entirety, and therefore can never, except by enthusiasm, be separated from this word." This dialectic of Word and Spirit was drawn from Luther; it fairly begs the question of its grounding in trinitarian theology—precisely

## Neo-Orthodoxy and the Renewal of Trinitarianism

the task undertaken by the postwar second generation of Neo-Orthodox Lutheran theology.

Even though Bonhoeffer's work in the Bethel Confession did not see the light of day in the time for which it was intended, his contention in it for the dialectical unity of Word and Spirit in an expressly hermeneutical approach to Scripture as witness, and to theology as contemporary interpretation for the sake of concrete, public proclamation and confession, put its diagnostic finger on the deep problems besetting the Lutheran tradition in theology. Accordingly Bonhoeffer's diagnosis, if not the text of the Bethel Confession, bore fruit in the postwar reassessment. For some, business continued as usual. But painful awareness of the paralysis of most of the church, the heresy of the German Christians and the weak political resistance of the confessing church catalyzed a renewal of systematic theology in the tradition of Luther by way of the retrieval of the ancient doctrine of the Trinity.

This can be seen especially in the leading theologians of the era: the Germans Wolfhart Pannenberg and Eberhard Jüngel and the American Robert Jenson. Each of these theologians excavated the deep trinitarianism underlying Luther's dialectical relationship of the Father's Word and Spirit because this doctrine of God grounds and clarifies the distinction-in-unity of law and gospel in God's history with humanity, enacted and thus represented by Israel and Israel's Jesus. Since the doctrine of the Trinity was not itself a matter of contention during the schism of the sixteenth century, it had been taken for granted on both sides. On examination, however, the reformation of doctrine inaugurated by Luther's theology of the cross exhibited deep tension with the overemphasis on the simplicity of perfect being in medieval scholastic theology. Unfortunately this tension has too often been simplistically expressed with the help of Bonhoeffer's statement from prison that "only a suffering God can help." One-sided emphasis on divine suffering, motivated by an apologetic concern to side with victims, however, only divinizes, even eternalizes the suffering creation. If God suffers, he suffers in order to overcome suffering; if God suffers it is not the pathetic suffering which befalls creatures but a truly divine, creative act of suffering compassion and solidarity on behalf of others which delivers them. What is at stake in the revision of the doctrine of God by the theology of the cross is not an affirmation of abject divine suffering, but affirmation of divine being whose glory is to come down into the depths, even to the depths of hell, in order to set its denizens free. The affirmation needed is not of a generic divine suffering, but of the trinitarian complexity of the eternal being of the God of love: the Father who sends the Son to suffer creation's travail in order to gain the redemption of our bodies. The oneness of God is not a metaphysical insight such as the classic doctrine of simplicity pretends to, but a rule stipulating that true God is the one who is rigorously conceived as the Creator of all that is not God.[6]

It is in this respect, too, especially the christological stress by Luther on the unity of person pressed hard against the metaphysical doctrine of divine simplicity—an emphasis which recurred especially in later Reformed Orthodoxy. Manifestly, a robust trinitarianism by which divine unity is apprehended in terms of the perichoresis of the three underlies Luther's theology as is evident in the following marginal gloss on Augustine already from his student days: "I, unless blessed Augustine would say otherwise, but I would say, that the Father is not the Father except from the Son, that is, from filiation. Thus neither by Himself is He wise, but through the Son who is His wisdom by which He is wise. Neither

6. See further, Hinlicky, *Divine Simplicity*.

by Himself is He good, but though the Holy Spirit who is His goodness. Thus it is that whenever He is called powerful, wise, good, always at the same time all three persons are named. The reason is because 'father' is relative. And, as Ambrose says here, He is not able to be named or called Father, unless the Son is also co-named. Thus being wise and wisdom are relative. And He is not able to be named such, unless the Son also is co-named."[7]

Luther's robust trinitarianism continues to undergird his theology throughout the reformer's career. It can be seen not only in his catechisms (his preferred form for the presentation of Christian doctrine) but also in his late-in-life composition of doctoral theses for students to defend (showing appreciation for the logical rigor achieved in scholastic disputation).[8] Above all, Luther's significant personal "confession of faith" in the Trinity appeared at the conclusion of his major christological treatise, *Confession concerning Christ's Supper*, which statement, according to Wilhelm Maurer, provided the template for the composition of the Augsburg Confession, undergirding its ecumenical intention. So the postwar renewal of trinitarianism could justly appeal to Luther, not least in order to ground the anti-enthusiastic dialectic of Word and Spirit and thus to anchor the law-gospel distinction in the one God's complex operations in judging, redeeming, and fulfilling the world on which the cross of Jesus stood.

Acknowledging Barth's new beginning for postmodern theology by pointing to the doctrine of the Trinity as the distinctively Christian thing to say about God, Pannenberg nonetheless sharply criticized Barth for his still too

---

7. My translation from Randbemerkung Luthers to the Sentences of Peter Lombard, Part 9. In *D. Martin Luthers Werke* [hereafter WA], 1:38.

8. Bielfeldt et al., *Substance of Faith*.

Western reliance on the psychological model of the Trinity as faculties at work in the unitary self-consciousness of a single intellect. This psychological model—"thought thinking and willing itself"—derives from Neoplatonism with its doctrine of the absolute One that thinks itself and wills itself, the latter two resulting in subordinate replicas of the first by which it is related to the created world of plurality and change. Against this Western tendency to reiterate neo-Platonic idealism under the guise of the ecumenical doctrine of the Trinity, Pannenberg argued that the Father, Son, and Holy Spirit appear in the Bible "as living realizations of separate centers of action,"[9] i.e., as agents in society "in such a way that each of the three persons relates to the others as others and distinguishes itself from them." Hence "[r]elations among the three persons that are defined as mutual self-distinction cannot be reduced to the relations of origin in the traditional sense. The Father does not merely beget the Son. He also hands over his kingdom to him and receives it back from him. The Son is not merely begotten of the Father. He is also obedient to him and he thereby glorifies him as the one God. The Spirit is not just breathed. He also fills the Son and glorifies him in his obedience to the Father, thereby glorifying the Father himself."[10] Pannenberg did not reject the distinction that comes by relation to origin, i.e., the "monarchy of the Father," but rather to the way that it becomes in Barth a surrogate for the One Subject enacting his subjectivity by the modes of his self-objectification and self-communication—a model too reminiscent of Hegelian idealism and its (mis-)interpretation of the doctrine of the Trinity along the lines of

9. Pannenberg, *Systematic Theology*, 1:319. For a more detailed treatment of Pannenberg, Jenson, and Jüngel from which this discussion is drawn, see Hinlicky, *Beloved Community*, 108–34.

10. Pannenberg, *Systematic Theology*, 1:320.

a modernized and historicized Neoplatonism. In place of this psychological model, Pannenberg finds the unity of the Three in the *perichoresis* or *circumincessio*, i.e., the "mutual indwelling" of the Three as articulated in the high priestly prayer of John 17, such that agency itself is mutually entailing cooperation among the Three with the implication, as we have just seen, that the Spirit and the Son also act upon the Father as upon each other.[11]

Pannenberg's is strong a trinitarian personalism, as we might call this understanding that personal individuality is constituted in the social mutuality of the three: this Father cannot be the Father that he is apart from this Son, nor can this Son be the Son that he is apart from this Father, nor can the Father and the Son so relate to each other apart from the Spirit who binds them in love, nor can the Spirit be the Holy Spirit that he is except as the Spirit of the Father and the Son in their mutual love. In this eternally circulating divine life of joyful exchanges, God is God for God, and so it is possible that this God as he truly is also becomes truly God for us in creation, its redemption and fulfillment.

Possible, not necessary! The social Trinity as an eternally beloved community (as I like to put it) undertakes a free action of love for community with creatures; God's history with humanity is not the display of a narcissistic egoism which needs a created world in order to work out its own identity, as Pannenberg puts it against Hegel: the "development of an absolute subject after the pattern of self-consciousness," the "logically necessary self-development of the Absolute in producing a world of the finite."

11. Harrison, "Perichoresis in the Greek Fathers," 53–65. A notable contribution of this study is Harrison's correlation of perichoresis with the ubiquitous and immediate presence of God *in creatio continua* in strong distinction from the Neo-Platonic scheme in which a mediating Logos is required to bridge the gap between transcendent Deity and the creaturely world.

So Pannenberg targets precisely the heterodoxy of Hegel's account of the Trinity,[12] according to which God is driven by lack, by the need to acquire a missing self-consciousness over against the otherness of creatures, with the result that God unfolds by way of a self-emptying kenosis. As left-wing Hegelians quickly realized, it is but a short step from here to the virtually atheistic result that unfolded Trinity in time is identical to humanity coming to its true self in the absolute consciousness of its identity as God. There is in Hegel a "kenotic collapse" in which God dissolves into enlightened humanity and humanity arises to its divine vocation to do what in unenlightened times it had expected God to do for it. While Hegel himself disguised this virtual atheism with ambiguous language, it is clear today that what he was actually saying was that in the beginning there was the undifferentiated Father, so to speak, who was not other than nothingness. Thus to acquire distinctiveness the Father estranged himself and became finite and other as the Son. The finite but estranged Son, representing creation, at last realized his unity with all and so became the Spirit, the world achieving self-consciousness as God incarnate.

The atheistic interpretation of the Christian Trinity in Hegel's footsteps, forcefully argued by Alexandre Kojeve,[13] is today powerfully voiced by the Marxist philosopher Slavoj Žižek: for him, the Spirit, arising from Christ's defeat at Golgotha after the realization that he was abandoned there because there was no heavenly Father to rescue him, now lives on in the militant (but endlessly ironic and thus impotent) revolutionary community. As Cyril O'Regan has shown, this entire reading of trinitarianism is predicated upon a Gnostic theology of divine neediness that derives

12. Ayres, *Nicea and Its Legacy*, 384–429.
13. Kojeve, *Introduction to the Reading of Hegel*.

in part from the Pietist mystic, Jacob Boehme.[14] It depends on the dialectical power of the negative endlessly to destabilize whatever has hitherto achieved any fixity. Cast into the terms of philosophical theology, "God" is driven by neediness to negate itself as an abstract, otherworldly idea by becoming wholly materialized. "God" awakens from this utter self-alienation as matter when matter awakens in "absolute consciousness" to its own identity as "God." By contrast we can say that robust trinitarianism proceeds from the positive dialectic of generosity; "to be God is to give (Latin: *esse Deum dare*)," as Luther often put it. Concretely, as Luther loved to say, above and beyond all temporal gifts God has given his very self in the person of his Son in the self-surpassing act of achieving a merciful righteousness on behalf of the lost and unworthy.

As Pannenberg points out, however, "if we think of the life of the Trinity in terms of the mutuality of the relations of the trinitarian persons, no such necessity [as Hegel imagines, for the Absolute to acquire self-consciousness via kenosis] arises. For each of the persons, self-distinction from the others is a condition of their fellowship in the unity of the divine life . . . Thus the divine life is a self-enclosed circle, which needs no other outside itself."[15] Because God is eternally the Trinity of love, God is not needy nor is God greedy. To be this God is freely to give, out of infinite abundance, for God and so also for us. Thus the potential for a revision of the hyper-simplicity interpretation of divine ontology in Luther's frequent dictum, to be God is to give, is taken up and actualized. The Johannine statement, "God is love," is rendered understandable not as a sentimental human projection but rigorously as divine ontology. The world accordingly is

14. O'Regan, *Heterodox Hegel*.
15. Pannenberg, *Systematic Theology*, 2:28–29, emphasis added.

not God's ego-trip—which is in fact Hegel's melodramatic mask for the apotheosis of the Cartesian-Kantian sovereignty of the modern self. The world is not the instrument by which God achieves self-consciousness, nor is history the process by which creatures become aware of their divinity. But the world is God's beloved creation fallen and in travail yet on the way to redemption and fulfillment in the Beloved Community which in the end comes as God's sharing of true and eternal life with creatures other than himself. Thus, over against Hegel and Žižek, we see how it is precisely trinitarianism, not the mere theism of perfect being metaphysics or the dynamic Unitarianism of Neoplatonism, which rises today as the Christian response to the challenge of contemporary atheism, showing in the process that much contemporary atheism is a perfectly Christian disbelief in idols posing as true God. Indeed, we may dialectically affirm the atheistic critique of the theistic idol of timeless eternity and perfect being as a step on the way towards the renewal of robust trinitarianism.[16]

Robert Jenson similarly advocated the theological revision of classical metaphysics with its a priori interpretation of God as protologically perfect being. He called for a critique of such "metaphysics of persistence" by an eschatological "metaphysics of anticipation," thus rejecting the merely theistic idea that what makes God divine is changeless self-identity or metaphysical simplicity. The claim for this doctrine is that it protects the aseity of God. But this claim to protect aseity is also made by the Cappadocians in teaching the "monarchy of the Father," i.e., that the unbegotten Father is the font of the deity who anticipates his own future precisely by generating the Son and breathing the Spirit. Jenson reclaims the latter way and in place of a locus on divine unity offers a locus on "patrology." The

16. See further Hinlicky, "Luther's Atheism."

metaphysics of persistence takes perfect being as its necessary being eternally grounding the changing and contingent beings immersed in time and bound by space. God's job here is metaphysical grounding. Consequently any hint of change in God quite literally shifts the ground beneath the creature's feet and threatens the cosmos with destabilization. But disruption of the fallen creation by the free advent of grace is exactly what the God of the gospel does as the gospel presents the One sent by his Father to break into a closed and self-referential system to bind up the strong man and plunder his goods; who comes to seek and find by the Spirit creatures who were not seeking but had rather gone astray and become captive. Found by God's disruptive grace, they may now in turn disruptively anticipate the God who promises to make all things new.

This God "of the future" is also believed to be the origin and continuing Creator and preserver of the created world which from its origin is destined for a future. But the created world is not taken by Jenson as a fixed stage of nature on which a subsequent history would play out. Rather following Karl Barth's revision of the doctrine of election, creation is taken as a reality which anticipates the reign of God, destined from the beginning for redemption and fulfillment. This metaphysics of anticipation does not jettison the eternity of God but reconceives it along the lines of the high priestly prayer of John 17, as the oneness in love that Jesus has had with his Father from the beginning but now petitions to extend to his disciples in time. The God of the gospel is in this way believed to be "eternal"—otherwise the Incarnation and the sending of the Spirit would be notions from nowhere and any sense of salvation as the redemption and fulfillment of the creation beyond its immanent possibilities would be lacking a competent agent. We would be left with process metaphysics and God as our fellow sufferer.

But for Jenson, even though he is very concerned not to open up a gap between the ontological and the economic Trinity, it may be said that the eternal Trinity as the divine way of being backs the economic Trinity as the divine way of engaging to redeem and fulfill the creation from origin on to eschaton. The difficulty that arises here—how God's eternity is to be conceived, if not as timelessness—is one that particularly vexed Jenson's post-modern theology.

Jenson's solution is to make the Trinity subject of the predicate, "one true God" (that is, not taking "one true God" as a fourth entity, such as perfect being or divine nature, as if a subject over against the Three in and as their mutual relations). Thus when the Father of the Son in the Spirit is the subject which governs the predicate, eternity, we see that eternity cannot be conceived by way of the pure negation of the temporally wrought and temporally terminated creature, as, then, some abstract opposite of time, as sheer timeless, hence motionless, hence spaceless self-identity, we know not what. As Trinity, there is sequence as also alterity in the eternal God: the unbegotten Father begets, the Son is begotten, and the Father of the Son breathes his Spirit on the Son so that in the Spirit the Son returns glory to the Father—and so the one God lives in this endless circulation ad infinitum. This is eternity conceived as "infinite temporal duration"—"God everlasting" as Nicholas Wolterstorff would put it. The Trinity is this "temporally infinite" (Jenson) going out and return, a divine motion or dance (*perichoresis*), hence time-like and space-like.[17] Just so the Trinity is the fittingly unbounded or infinite being of the Creator of a time and place for creatures. "To be God is always to be open to and always to open a future, transgressing all past-imposed conditions."[18]

17. Jenson, *Systematic Theology*, 214–18.
18. Jenson, *Systematic Theology*, 216.

We learn this "revision of metaphysics" from the redemptive and fulfilling missions of the Son and Spirit because these show that the same eternal God and Father is not bound to the origin nor to be located back there as First Cause and thus understood in time as the perpetuator of things by means of so-called secondary causes. Rather the very eternal God and Father is from the beginning free to innovate in accord with his original intention to redeem the fallen world of creatures for a fulfillment that had been forfeited. "Consider not the former things, nor consider the things of old. Behold, I am doing a new thing!" "If anyone is in Christ, behold! New creation!" "And He who sat upon the throne declared, 'Behold! I make all things new!'"

In the Bible, it is such works of saving novelty that raise the insignia of true deity (Romans 4: 17). The God of the gospel is not bound slavishly to the past, even God's own past, but is self-surpassing freedom. In accentuating this, Jenson is appealing to notable statements of Luther about the deity of the one true God, Creator of all that is not God. For Luther creation out of nothing (Latin: *ex nihilo*) is the insignia of the one true God, not, as we have heard, in the sense of a once and for all act at the origin setting up a stable stage on which to perform a salvation history but rather as continuous action in which the Creator God, faithful to his own good purpose, ever innovates in a true history, inclusive of natural history, with creatures for their redemption and fulfillment.

Here we see that the power of God includes the Father's freedom to entrust his reign to the Son and the Spirit, just as the Son's freedom had been to abandon himself to his Father's vindication, as now the Spirit's freedom is to glorify the Father in the Son by making this God possible for the dying sinners which believers are and remain in their organic solidarity with the common body of fallen humanity on the earth. Hence divine power is not having no further possibilities as the already perfect being who, having decreed once and for all, now gazes serenely upon creation as it unfolds necessarily. Divine omnipotence consists rather in having all possibilities available on the way to the coming of the kingdom. Wisdom is not using any and all possibilities but only those that creatively love. Love is not realizing all one's own possibilities but surrendering some to another in generating the daily miracle of trust, the glue of mutuality in beloved community.

The Father trusts the Son to obey; the Son trusts the Father to vindicate; the Spirit of the Father and the Son entrusts believers with his temple, the earthly body of the risen Lord. In these actions of personal fidelity, the Trinity is the free subject of its own divine predicates, not the slave of any one of them. The "who" determines the "what" and the "how" and this "who" is not determined by any pre-conceived definition or mechanism. Instead, if we think this way about what makes God God for us, it is the Father's free self-determination to redeem and fulfill the creation by the missions of the Son and the Spirit. The eternal harmony of power, wisdom, and love, the divine attributes appropriated respectively to the almighty Father, the Incarnate Word, and the life-breathing Spirit, will be revealed by the coming of the Reign in power and glory and in just this way demonstrate the triune God's creation of all that is not God as God becomes all things to all people (1 Corinthians 15:28).

Criticism recognizes parallels in Jenson to Hegel's philosophy and is it indeed the case that in some respects Jenson's system betrays affinity with German idealism; but unless the mere utilization of non-biblical terminology-cum-conceptuality is shown specifically to obscure theological reading of the scriptural canon in the light of its christological-soteriological key, such criticism is idle. It no more applies to the classical theological appropriation of Platonism in the two-natures doctrine as a defense against Gnosticism than it applies to post-Christendom appropriation of Hegelianism to distinguish the God of the gospel from the God of the philosophers—a purpose subversive of Hegel's own intention. Arguably, even in its heterodoxy, Hegelianism reflects centuries of Christian impact upon the philosophical tradition in a way that Platonism could not have.

It is, however, Jüngel not Jenson who is frequently but most unfairly dismissed as a latter-day Hegelian by complacent and/or nostalgic theologians unwilling to face as courageously as he the contemporary human experience of the "death of God" in the post-Christendom culture of the West. Let us repeat for emphasis the insight going back to Luther's theology of the cross with its profound critique of the theology of glory that to believe in the God of the gospel is to disbelieve the idols, even if not especially the refined and influential Christian-Platonic idol of abstract theism. Theism is the reification of a "no-thing," the god whom Nietzsche rightly proclaimed dead. It posits a baseline perfect being theology with the Christian additions of the Son and the Spirit for those so inclined, in the process turning the Father into the purely negative notion of the unbegotten. Trinitarianism denies, however, that there is any true God but the Father of the Son on whom he breathes his Spirit; it is atheistic, then, with respect to the idols of the nations, crude or sophisticated, which have no real existence.

Jüngel's trinitarianism correlates *positively* with much modern atheism in its disbelief in perfect being theology. In this engagement, Jüngel found a precedent in Luther who acknowledged the powerful temptation to atheism at the conclusion of his treatise on bound choice in his discussion of the theological darkness of the "light of nature." This darkness of the hidden God Luther interpreted as tempting to the sin of despair. For all its superficial, anthropocentric optimism, is not despair lurking just below the surface of emergent postmodernity? To be sure, the present is populated with publicity hound public atheists indiscriminately attacking all things religious, Christian and/or theological. Rarely is the Nietzschean burden of atheism openly acknowledged, let alone honestly embraced. After Hitler, Hiroshima, and Stalin, nihilism has indeed disclosed the metaphysics of our time.

Jüngel's magnificent study, *God as the Mystery of the World* bears the subtitle, *On the Foundation of the Theology of the Crucified One in the Dispute between Theism and Atheism*.[19] This profound work interpreted the despairing modern experience of the "death of God" as the deserved collapse of perfect being theism in the wake of Europe's woeful twentieth-century experience of massive criminality and incalculable death. Thus there is at least this much of a parallel with Hegel in the latter's argument that the abstract idea of God dies in the human experience of awakening to self-consciousness at its own bloodied hands. But at this juncture any affinity ends since for Hegel this awakening led to supreme human self-confidence, while for postmodern people it is Nietzsche's overwhelming vertigo, ever spiraling down into an abyss of despair. There is no hope we can believe in.

Christian theology in the tradition of Luther can be resolutely historicist in metaphysics, for as Bultmann pointed out, no one can create their own worldview; it is rather something given to them by history. The supposition, that

19. Jüngel, *God as the Mystery of the World*. Jüngel's student, Ingolf U. Dalferth continues in his teacher's train in *Crucified and Resurrected*.

## Neo-Orthodoxy and the Renewal of Trinitarianism

if only we could get our metaphysics right, theology would take care of itself, is nostalgia for a golden age that never was. Theology is forced back today in this era of metaphysical postmodernism and theological post-Christendom on to its own two feet—the gospel and the Bible.

But this is no disadvantage. For Jüngel it recalls theology to the one true God who, out of creative love, joins the divine self to the creature's real experience of death, including the death of meaning—also the macro-meaning that once hung on the grounding apprehension of perfect being. Simple theism in any case is inadequate to parse the movement of divine and creative agape-love which the gospel narrates according to Luther's theology of the cross. "God," taking this *title* (for the one and true God as the one Creator of all that is not God) as if a single subject and personal name, either lives or dies and cannot be both at once, although just this "paradox" is precisely what the theology of the cross requires to be proclaimed and understood. Trinitarian personalism is needed to parse the dynamic, for sequenced, simultaneity of Good Friday and Easter morn: not only the solidarity of divine and creative love with the perishing creature but also the victory of divine and creative love on behalf of the dying sinner, powerful to draw life from death.

Thus Jüngel is able to interpret *theologically* the central mystery of the gospel—the resurrection of the crucified Jesus—when he explains how the Spirit raises Jesus, shrouded in the sin and death of the world, anew to the Father's embrace, such that the Father now recognizes in his crucified and risen Son his own love for the lost. This reconciliation of the Father and the Son by the Spirit within the life of God is the deepest basis for the reconciliation of the holy God and the sinful creature. The confrontation between God the Father and God the Son on Golgotha is reconciled by God the Holy Spirit in the achievement of a new relationship to creation.

The logic involved in this account is surely one that cannot rest content with the static binary of the law of non-contradiction, which must interpret predications like "Christ crucified" or "God incarnate" as either errors or nonsense. It is crucial to realize that in his case against the prison house of Aristotelian logic, Jüngel, following Luther, is precisely not arguing for sloppy appeal to metaphor, symbol, or analogy. That appeal is still made by the basically apophatic theology stemming from Platonism to warrant a vague, nonliteral discourse affirming a divine something we know not what, yet glimpsed in representations purporting to show us what God is like. Instead Jüngel is arguing for metaphor as catachresis. Catachresis is the rhetorical figure of an apparent contradiction, hence of a "paradox," for the purpose of registering a new meaning in the world for which there is no existing vocabulary.[20] In this Jüngel is drawing expressly upon Luther's view of the "new language of the Spirit."[21] As Luther wrote in his treatise against Latomus, Paul's statement that "Christ was made to be sin" denotes a startling new thing in the world, for it is "not only a metaphor of words but of things. For truly our sins are transferred from us and placed on Him, so that all who believe Him truly have no sins but they are transferred onto Him, absorbed in Him, no longer damning him."[22] Like the cognate paradoxes "Christ crucified" or "This is my body" or "the Word made flesh," "Christ made to be

---

20. Biblical metaphor specifies "*in what way* God is . . ." God, apart from which there is "no proper talk of God." Jüngel, *Theological Essays I*, 45–46.

21. See Anna Vind's and my own treatment of Luther on metaphor in Bayer and Gleede, eds., *Creator est Creatura*, 95–124, 147–66.

22 WA 8:87, my translation; cf. *Against Latomus* in LW 32:200.

sin" gives expression to a new reality for which no previous vocabulary or conceptual reality is available.

To be sure, for Luther, the exchange *of things* concerns in the first place Christ, not the believer, as the new reality thus indicated by the paradoxical rhetoric: Christ is the new reality who came as the Lamb of God to take away the sin of the world and once and for all accomplished just this redemptive exchange. Only so, however, can this new reality presently speak and thus regard its auditor as likewise exchanged and thus forgiven and freed as a matter of truth, no matter how she feels one way or another. Luther's "exchange of things" (Latin: *metaphora rerum*) concerns Christ who comes to the sinner as the Lamb of God.

A question that remains is whether this power to become the child of God comes about in the believer merely by saying so, "abracadabra," that is, as some "radically Lutheran" contemporary theologies "of the Word" seem to insist—apart, that is, from the "translating" work of the Spirit of God who brings Christ to the believer in word and sacrament and brings the believer to Christ by the generation of trusting faith. To be sure, this would be none other than the Spirit of Jesus Christ, whom the Son breathes upon the auditor in exchange for her doubt and despair. To speak here combining Pauline and Johannine idioms: the Spirit sheds the love of God abroad in human hearts which have been convicted concerning sin, and righteousness, and judgment. Then it is in the Spirit-given reality of faith which works a corresponding new reality in the sinner who thus yields sin to Christ and in turn appropriates his righteousness as her own. This Spirit-given *translatio rerum* derivatively but all the same truly pertains to the human subject. The faith that justifies in its own *specific way of being* thus corresponds in reality to the *specific way of being*

## LUTHERAN THEOLOGY

that is told by the catachrestic metaphor, Christ crucified for our sins but raised for our justification.

The gospel word, according to Jüngel, works as catachrestic metaphor *in an ordered sequence* as we saw in Luther's critique of enthusiasm. It thus passes from paradox to simile, from contradiction to similitude, from the death of the sinner to the new-born child of God renewed in the image of God for likeness to God. In this Luther's crucial purpose clause, "God kills *in order to* make alive," is at work. Another way to pose the question about how Jüngel thinks this purposeful movement occurs is to ask, "Can the catachrestic metaphor fail in this progression, e.g., can it blind and harden (Mark 4:11-12) rather than enlighten and redeem?" Arguably, it *can* fail in the sequence Jüngel, following Luther, intends, precisely if and when the disruptive metaphor of paradox is Spiritlessly thought to work "on its own," so to speak, automatically. In this case the metaphor has to be taken as sheer nonsense and deliberate absurdity—Tertullian's *credo quia absurdum est* (Latin: I believe because it is absurd). This sometimes seems to be the claim of modern champions of the "monergism" of the Word.

But the cost of this construction of deliberate absurdity is enormous: the Word is thought to work on its own when the dissonant sting of paradox is muted by obliterating the offensive *intelligibility* provided by theological interpretation of the catachrestic metaphor. The opposite defanging typical of the liberal tradition turns paradox into mere simile: somehow the death of Christ shows us what God is like. But this is a dead-end. Little wonder that today feminist and liberation theologians protest such a sadistic simile: it was not the God of love who crucified Christ but us! Just so, however, the very point about the God of love who spared not his own Son but gave him up for us all is lost in confusion because the intended progression *through*

## Neo-Orthodoxy and the Renewal of Trinitarianism

*contradiction* to similitude is obscured. In this case, if not taken *in the Spirit by faith* as the contradiction in terms, "Christ crucified," this kerygma has to be taken *out of the Spirit, in bad faith*, disclosing some alleged truth like, "To be Christ is to be victim," or "The victims of the world are Christ." Not a little contemporary theology, right and left, views the matter in this perverse way.

But it is important to see why we may come to such perverse theology that divinizes victimization or victimizes the divine—and justly offends alike those who struggle against victimization and those who hope in God's vindication of victims. We mute the paradox in this way, making it into an illuminating disclosure of some supposedly deeper truth of our world, because we take ourselves, the human auditors of this strange announcement, as having by the mere light of nature epistemic access and corresponding aptitude to process this gospel information in comparison to, and thus as part of, all that we already know. We have access and acquire aptitude as members of a system of things who regularly learn the lesser known in terms of what is already familiar. We presume to learn accordingly what it is to be Christ crucified by our all too familiar experience of victimization. "Christ crucified"—for good or ill, victimization is the deepest truth of our world. Self-hatred or other-hatred, as the history of popular Christianity amply documents, becomes the religious work that brings us close to the divine.

Alongside of these three giants of post-war Neo-Orthodox Lutheran theology, Oswald Bayer, Carl Braaten, and Kazoh Kitamori must also be mentioned at the conclusion of this chapter. Of all of these theologians, Bayer has been without doubt the most intentionally "Lutheran," though not in a neo-confessionalist way. Bayer's project is the re-presentation of Luther's own theology as a contemporary possibility. That gives his theology a depth, though it comes at the expense of the breadth of our three major figures. Indeed, the American theologian, Mark Mattes, published a study[23] that positioned Bayer's project against Jenson, Pannenberg, Jüngel (and the Reformed Moltmann) on the grounds that only Bayer made, so to speak, a systematic "anti-system" principle of Luther's distinction between law and gospel. Mattes was on to something here in that Bayer declined the modern genre of "systematic" theology undertaken by Jenson, Pannenberg, and Jüngel on the grounds that it forced an artificial harmonization upon the contradictory imports of the law as threatening, divine demand which reveals sin and accuses sinners on the one side and of the gospel on the other side as comforting, divine promise which reveals mercy and forgives sinners. Theology itself, Bayer argued, must live in this abiding tension between two words of God until the light of glory dawns.

The tension within God's Word between holy demand and holy promise resists systematization this side of the eschaton. Systematization imposes an artificial unity on a gap between the word which condemns and the word which pardons which human thinking—especially manifest in its totalitarian desire for systematic coherence—cannot and should not prematurely close. Consequently Bayer wrote theology in the interventionist genres of historical studies, discrete monographs, and essays (much like an American Lutheran soulmate, Robert W. Bertram, who never published a monograph, let alone a system of theology, but made penetrating interventions speaking to the theology of culture, razor-sharp indictments of the fundamentalist turn of his Lutheran Church-Missouri Synod, sympathetic but critical responses to the emergence of liberation theologies and solid contributions to the Lutheran-Roman Catholic

23. Mattes, *The Role of Justification in Contemporary Theology*.

## Neo-Orthodoxy and the Renewal of Trinitarianism

dialogue). That being said, it is too reductive to pigeonhole Bayer in this way as a mere essayist or for that matter Jenson, Pannenberg, and Jüngel as obsessive systematizers.

As our discussion of Bonhoeffer's treatment of the law-gospel distinction in the Bethel Confession has shown, theology in the tradition of Luther must learn from experience—especially from the particularly galling experience of pro-Nazi German Christianity's abuse of the law-gospel *distinction* to expunge the Old Testament as a literature of Judaic works-righteousness and to redraw Jesus of Galilee as an Aryan Jew-fighter, figuring a heroic antinomian battle to restore the innocence of becoming and attain a new order beyond good and evil. Luther's unification of law and gospel with the purpose clause, as in "God kills *in order to* make alive," is as well-grounded historically as his insistence upon a proper distinction (not a dualistic antagonism) between holy demand and all-the-more holy, for surpassing, gift of the righteousness which meets, satisfies, and thus overcomes magnificently the law's condemnation.

In any case Bayer's great contribution to Neo-Orthodox Lutheran theology has been his deep exploration of the motif of "promise" as a performative utterance in which the utterer of a promise puts forth his own self, in the form of his public reputation, in order to enable a trusting response. This is not abracadabra. There is self-giving in the action of making of a promise. A promise delivers the promiser to the addressee, even if the promise is otherwise not yet fulfilled in fullness. On analysis, then, promise-trusting entails definite beliefs about the promiser, namely that the promiser acts with goodwill and that the promiser is competent to deliver the goods. Thus definite beliefs about God attend divine promise and the creature's existential trust. In light of this analysis, Bayer recommends a renewed "catechetical" theology to articulate the knowledge of God for us today.

Thus, while Bayer eschews the academic construction of a "system" of theology and avoids equally the dogmatic overreach of Lutheran Orthodoxy, he does venture a suitable form for the presentation of Christian beliefs in catechesis. Wary of the whole lot of German idealists, Bayer might be understood to be closer to their existentialist critic, Soren Kierkegaard, though Bayer has in fact identified the anti-Kantian gadfly, Johann Georg Hamann, as Christian light shining in the particular darkness which is the assertion of the sovereign self in Cartesian-Kantian modernity.[24]

Carl Braaten is another second-generation Neo-Orthodox Lutheran theologian worthy of mention. He was by far regarded as the leading Lutheran theologian in the United States in the latter half of the twentieth century, publishing extensively and treating a rich spectrum of topics not easily summarized or synthesized: the problem of the historical Jesus and the Christ of faith, the postwar rise of political and liberation theologies, Tillich's method of correlation, the rediscovery of eschatology and the thought of Pannenberg. Later in life, he immersed himself in the ecumenical doctrinal dialogues that were generated by the Second Vatican Council. Together with his partner, Robert Jenson, with whom he had co-edited the once influential journal, *dialog*, he founded the Center for Catholic and Evangelical theology devoted to the doctrinal reconciliation of Christian traditions intending orthodoxy. With Jenson he had also edited a collaborative, but decidedly mixed-bag *Christian Dogmatics* for seminary instruction in the Evangelical Lutheran Church in America, a merger in 1989 of two-thirds of American Lutheranism in which the nineteenth-century theology of liberal Lutheranism has since enjoyed a considerable renaissance.

---

24. Bayer, *Contemporary in Dissent*.

## Neo-Orthodoxy and the Renewal of Trinitarianism

As a student of Tillich's, Braaten was always keen to analyze the cultural situation and correlate its questions with the Christian message, understood as the gospel of the resurrection of the crucified Jesus anticipating the coming reign of God. Braaten was the son of missionary parents in Madagascar, an upbringing never far from his consciousness. Thus perhaps the most enduring contribution of Braaten was his re-conceptualization of the church as mission, where mission is theologically grounded in the complex relationships of the triune God with the fallen creation on the way to its redemption and fulfillment.[25] His student, Cheryl Peterson, has published a study on ecclesiology which synthesizes these concerns for mission in pneumatology.[26]

"God has died! If this does not startle us, what will? The church must keep this astonishment alive. The church ceases to exist when she loses this astonishment." It is fitting to conclude this chapter on the several forms taken in twentieth-century Neo-Orthodox Lutheran theology with the Japanese Kazoh Kitamori, an interesting but complicated figure who has been more exploited by theological revisionists or condemned as a heretical "patripassionist," than seriously understood. The title of his signature work, *Theology of the Pain of God*, has been hijacked in support of deconstructive briefs on behalf of a pathetic deity who feels the world's pain but can do little about it. But such a "kenotic collapse" is far from Kitamori's meaning.

Kitamori came to his theological task as a new Christian in Japan, particularly inspired by his Luther studies and consequently perplexed by the misleading truisms of the mere theism of the Western tradition of Christian Platonism. Precisely as newcomer and cultural outsider, Kitamori perceived the deep theological contradiction

25. Braaten, *Flaming Center*.
26. Peterson, *Who Is the Church?*

between the touted apathy of the God of the philosophers and the pathos of the Bible's passionately engaged God—directly, according to his own testimony, in his reading of the book of Jeremiah.

Kitamori completed his signature treatise towards the end of the Second World War as the Japanese people faced the grief and humiliation of their impending defeat. In the traditional Kabuki theater of Japanese culture Kitamori saw the agony of parents who watched their children give their lives for the sake of their people; he thought that this very contemporary yet also deeply traditional Japanese experience could be captured by the gospel to build a communicative bridge for the evangelization of the defeated nation. Moreover, he argued that such a truly indigenous Japanese theology could offer to the ecumenical church an important corrective of the dominant Western tradition formed by Christian Platonism. But indigenization never meant for Kitamori renunciation and ignorance of the gospel's historical path through Western culture. A lesson rather to be learned especially by theologians in cultures where the gospel comes new is that gospel bearing news of the incarnation necessarily enculturates. Inevitably then when the same gospel passes on to any newcomers it comes with accumulated cultural baggage and it will acquire similar baggage in its new acculturation. The hard work is consequently required of critical appreciation and salient appropriation by relative newcomers. Kitamori in fact deeply immersed himself in the German Lutheran historical scholarship of the nineteenth century and, like Pannenberg, Jüngel, and Jenson, he knew in particular both the power and the danger for Christian theology of Hegelian idealism. In Kitamori all sorts of interesting, and for the global future of theology in Luther's tradition, important tendencies intersected.

## Neo-Orthodoxy and the Renewal of Trinitarianism

Kitamori's argument for the "pain of God" came by way of taking up Luther's dialectical conception of God, invoking the reformer's theme of the "mighty dual" of "God against God." What is at issue here is the merciful love of God for his creatures *and yet simultaneously* his righteous wrath of love against them as sinners ruining themselves and all creation under their dominion. These contradictory tendencies of the same love of God precipitate a genuine struggle within God's own life as the God of the Bible engages in a genuine and thus painful history with humanity. How can God love the unlovable—not just social or legal others on an immanent and horizontal plane, but the loveless ones who embrace lovelessness, thus on a vertical plane spiting the Creator God who is their source as also the source of their victims? Divine love for Luther's "real, not fictitious, sinners" is costly and painful love of enemies. "God himself was broken, was wounded, and suffered, because he embraced those who should not be embraced."[27]

In brief, *The Theology of the Pain of God* argues for a "pain" that is uniquely and specifically divine. This is the pain of God by which merciful love overcomes angry justice, yet not by the divine Fiat by a sheer act of will but rather by a costly satisfaction of justice for the sake of those unjust ones under its indictment. To say with theological liberalism that "God is love" settles little; it merely specifies that the one true God, Creator of all that is not God, cares for the creation as for his own precious work. But this very care of divine love can and does take the alien form of wrath against what is against love—against the serene and

---

27. Kitamori, *Theology of the Pain of God*, 22. In the foreword Anri Morimoto clarifies that where the English often says "embrace those who should not be embraced" the Japanese can also be translated as "embrace those who cannot be embraced." It is not only a moral but more profoundly an ontological issue.

indifferent apathy of the bystander, not to mention the deliberate cruelty of the perpetrator. A divine dilemma! Like the church father Athanasius, Kitamori's reading of the Hebrew prophets together with the New Testament required him to ask, What was God in his goodness to do, wanting neither to leave cruel sin unchecked, nor victims without vindication, nor to destroy precious creatures howsoever sinful in the process?

Of course, to grasp this question, one must with Kitamori adopt the perspective of the biblical prophets, such as Jeremiah; this prophetic perspective, bespeaking the Lord's controversy with his people, militates against any superstitious religious individualism which in any case would only employ God privately to avoid penalties and gain rewards. But the wrath of divine love is not petty like religious individualism. God's wrath is not a superstition that God executes personal vendettas. God's wrath is revealed from heaven against *all* ungodliness and wickedness of humanity and it is realized not by stray thunderbolts striking particular individuals but by abandoning corporate sin to its own social consequences which are ruin and death of the creation. Thus God's wrath is manifest (so Kitamori implies writing in 1944) in Japan's impending humiliation of defeat. The real question which arises from such analysis, just as in the biblical prophets, is whether there will be life after this death and mercy for these who are thus defeated. And the only deep answer to this question is the pain of God by which God takes upon himself well-merited wrath in the person of his crucified Son so that, satisfying justice, God moves justly beyond the wrath of his love to gain the triumph for the mercy of love.

It is notable that to articulate this drama of self-surpassing divine love, Kitamori must deploy trinitarian language, even as he must criticize in the process the fixed idea of static "natures" often presupposed both in Christology's doctrine of the "two natures in one person" as also in the crucial trinitarian distinction between nature and person. To be useful to Christian theology such philosophical terminology must be baptized! The pain of God can only finally be a message of salvation if at the cross God "continues to live in the person of the Father while dying in the person of the Son. The death of God the Son can be called the pain of God because the person of the Father lived. Pain can only be experienced by the living, not by the dead who are already freed from suffering . . . God the Father who hid himself in the death of God the Son is God in pain. Therefore the pain of God is neither merely the pain of God the Son, nor merely the pain of God the Father, but the pain of the two persons who are essentially one."[28] Thus Luther's more dialectical conception of God and the renewal of trinitarianism in Neo-Orthodox Lutheran theology dovetailed in a cultural context no longer undergirded or rather burdened with the platitudes of Christian Platonism.

---

28. Kitamori, *Theology of the Pain of God*, 115.

Conclusion

# A BRIEF PROLEGOMENA TO ANY FUTURE LUTHERAN THEOLOGY

AS A CONTEMPORARY LUTHERAN theologian, this author shares the concern of Karl Barth about the vulnerability of Lutheran theology to ideological captivity by the zeitgeist.[1] It is fitting to conclude this introduction by sketching the author's perspective on the contested contemporary world of Lutheran theology, riven between fundamentalisms and liberalisms, radicalisms and confessionalisms. This is also the case within the proliferation of "global Lutheranisms," as the younger churches in the Two-Thirds World spawned by the nineteenth-century missionary movement have matured to articulate Lutheran theologies of their own in diverse

1. Barth, "Introduction."

## A Brief Prolegomena to Any Future Lutheran Theology

social contexts quite other than those of decaying European or American Christendom. Neo-confessional Lutheranisms divide into self-described "word alone" and "evangelical catholic" wings while liberalism's ugly twin, fundamentalism, persists today in the circled wagon of a denominational Lutheranism, publicly aligning itself with "young earth" creationism, rejection of evolutionary biology and of historical criticism in biblical scholarship in a ludicrous claim to have achieved orthodoxy. Liberalism in Europe and America has experienced a significant resurgence, though it blends into perspectives of contemporary liberation and feminist theologies which in turn often thoroughly problematize historical Lutheran theology as surveyed in the preceding.

A salient illustration: for Luther the real threat of the righteous wrath of God is indispensable to his understanding of the gospel as news of the costly and surpassing love of God attaining mercy for real, not fictitious sinners in the course of an equally real history with them. Yet current liberation and feminist theologies—to paint with a broad brush—are often concerned to abolish just this theology of the costly "pain" of God (Kitamori) in actually loving enemies and to replace it with the picture of God without qualification siding with historical victims—albeit haplessly helpless to do much about it since God cannot be conceived to punish perpetrators. Much contemporary liberal Lutheran proclamation thus seems apologetically concerned to assure the traumatized that "God is not a problem" (as Sarah Hinlicky Wilson reported to me upon listening to Lutheran sermons for two years recently in the Twin Cities area). Yet Luther himself was concerned to proclaim only God and God alone as our true problem.

Giving the devil his due, to be sure, today's neo-liberals have good reason for wanting to disown one dreadful and deeply ingrained aspect of Luther's legacy that lays behind

Luther's own reckless dive into violent rhetoric against Pope, revolutionary agitators, and Jewish rabbis. The historical Luther's violent rhetoric in this regard provides plentiful cause for contemporary revisionism in wishing to leave behind once and for all his apocalyptically charged and resolutely dialectical discourse regarding God.

But it will not do simply to replace a bad idea of God with a good idea of God. By "theology," this introduction has meant "knowledge of God." In the present, theology as an academic discipline appears in diverse, often rival forms that give no special attention to knowledge of God. The paradigm descended from Immanuel Kant thus still remains in force. Kant, speaking for the Tribunal of Reason, banished knowledge of God from the field of rationality and in its place there arose a new paradigm of "religious studies"—knowledge, no longer of God, but of human representations of God. This change in subject matter is reflected especially in the modern academic division of labor between systematic, biblical, historical, and practical theologies—a disciplinary reorganization descending from Friedrich Schleiermacher, the significant post-Kantian theologian from the Reformed tradition who became the "father of Protestant liberalism." This division of labor reinforces, often unwittingly, the eclipse of knowledge of God in contemporary theology due to the divorce and increasing gulf between biblical scholarship and its historical and anthropological methods on the one side and so-called "constructive" theology on the other side. The reader should part from this book, then, reminded that the material selected for introducing the tradition of Christian theology stemming from Martin Luther has been governed by its against-the-stream contemporary relevance for the pursuit of the knowledge of God.

## A Brief Prolegomena to Any Future Lutheran Theology

If wonder at the pain of God surpassing God thus provides the depth of theology's knowledge of God in the tradition of Luther, trinitarianism provides its height. What is needed to broaden and horizontalize this height and depth for the future is the integration of the three predominant atonement motifs from the New Testament: liberation from anti-divine powers, the free and joyful new obedience of the liberated in discipleship to Jesus, and these two always on the basis of the sovereign reconciliation of the holy God with the sinner given in the resurrection of crucified Jesus as the ever gracious starting point, and never the uncertain goal, of the Christian life. As that integration of canonical soteriological accounts, so frequently and injuriously played off against one another in the history of Christian schism, is achieved, the twentieth-century notion of "beloved community" comes on the scene to replace the deadening, debilitating rivalries inherited from the schisms of the sixteenth century.

Beloved Community is figured in Jesus' high priestly prayer and eloquently described in 1 Corinthians 13. It was conceptualized by the obscure American philosopher Josiah Royce and preached powerfully to a nation reeking with racial injustice by the Rev. Dr. Martin Luther King Jr. Beloved Community moves the church into new forms of fellowship beyond its own broad but definite boundaries. Beloved Community as a concept mediates between the church visible and militant on the one side and the coming reign of God on the other. So enabled by it to discern signs of the Spirit's work in the world among sheep not of its own fold, the church and its theology may construct real if yet provisional alliances with all who would be motivated by the holy love of the unleashed Spirit of Jesus and his Father which in apocalyptic battle still must militate against what is against love.

# BIBLIOGRAPHY

Arndt, Johann. *True Christianity*. Translated by Peter Erb. Classics in Western Spirituality. New York: Paulist, 1979.

Ayres, Lewis. *Nicea and Its Legacy: An Approach to Fourth-Century Trinitarian Theology*. Oxford: Oxford University Press, 2006.

Barth, Karl. *Church Dogmatics*. II/2, *The Doctrine of God, Part Two*. Translated by G. W. Bromiley and T. F. Torrance. Edinburgh: T. & T. Clark, 1974.

———. *From Rousseau to Ritschl*. Translated by Brian Cozens. Library of Philosophy and Theology. London: SCM, 1959.

———. "Introduction." In *The Essence of Christianity*, by Ludwig Feuerbach, x–xxxii. Translated by George Eliot. Harper Torchbooks. New York: Harper, 1957.

Barth, Karl, and Rudolf Bultmann. *Letters 1922–1966*. Translated by Geoffrey W. Bromiley. Grand Rapids: Eerdmans, 1981.

Bartsch, Hans Werner, ed. *Kerygma and Myth*. New York: Harper & Row, 1961.

Bayer, Oswald. *A Contemporary in Dissent: Johann Georg Hamann as Radical Enlightener*. Translated by Roy A. Harrisville and Mark C. Mattes. Grand Rapids: Eerdmans, 2012.

———. *Martin Luthers Theologie: Eine Vergegenwaertigung*. 2nd ed. Tübingen: Mohr/Siebeck, 2004.

———. *Martin Luther's Theology: A Contemporary Interpretation*. Translated by Thomas H. Trapp. Grand Rapids: Eerdmans, 2007.

## Bibliography

Bayer, Oswald, and Benjamin Gleede, eds. *Creator est Creatura: Luthers Christologie als Lehre von der Idiomenkommunikation.* Theologische Bibliothek Topelmann 138. Berlin: de Gruyter, 2007.

Bergen, Doris L. *Twisted Cross: The German Christian Movement in the Third Reich.* Chapel Hill: University of North Carolina Press, 1996.

Bielfeldt, Dennis, et al. *The Substance of Faith: Luther on Doctrinal Theology.* Minneapolis: Fortress, 2008.

Bonhoeffer, Dietrich. *Dietrich Bonhoeffer: Berlin: 1932–1933.* Dietrich Bonhoeffer Works 12. Edited by Larry Rassmussen. Translated by Isabel Best and David Higgins. Minneapolis: Fortress, 2009.

Braaten, Carl E. *The Flaming Center: A Theology of Christian Mission.* 1977. Reprint, Eugene, OR: Wipf & Stock, 2016.

Brecht, Martin. *Martin Luther: Shaping and Defining the Reformation, 1521–1532.* Translated by J. L. Schaaf. Minneapolis: Fortress, 1990.

Brown, Dale W. *Understanding Pietism.* Rev. ed.. Nappanee, IN: Evangel, 1996.

Brunner, Emil. *The Christian Doctrine of God.* Dogmatics 1. Translated by Olive Wyon. Philadelphia: Westminster, 1974.

Bultmann, Rudolf. *Faith and Understanding.* Edited by Robert W. Funk. Translated by Louise Pettibone Smith. Philadelphia: Fortress, 1987.

Busch, Eberhard. *Karl Barth and the Pietists: The Young Karl Barth's Critique of Pietism and Its Response.* Translated by Donald W. Bloesch. Downers Grove, IL: InterVarsity, 2004.

Campbell, Ted A. *The Religion of the Heart: A Study of European Religious Life in the Seventeenth and Eighteenth Centuries.* Columbia: University of South Carolina Press, 1991.

Cassirer, Ernst. *The Philosophy of the Enlightenment.* Translated by F. C. A. Koelln and J. P. Pettegrove. Princeton: Princeton University Press, 1979.

Chemnitz, Martin. *The Two Natures of Christ.* Translated by J. A. O. Preus. St. Louis: Concordia, 1971.

Dalferth, Ingolf U. *Crucified and Resurrected: Restructuring the Grammar of Christology.* Translated by Jo Bennett. Grand Rapids: Baker Academic, 2015.

DeJonge, Michael P. *Bonhoeffer's Theological Formation: Berlin, Barth, & Protestant Theology.* Oxford: Oxford University Press, 2012.

Dieter, Theodor. *Der junge Luther und Aristoteles: Eine historisch-systematische Undersuchung zum Verhältnis von Theologie und*

*Philosophie*. Theologische Bibliothek Töpelmann 105. Berlin: de Gruyter, 2001.

Dillenberger, John. *God Hidden and Revealed: The Interpretation of Luther's deus absconditus and Its Significance for Religious Thought*. Philadelphia: Muhlenberg, 1953.

———. *Protestant Thought and Natural Science: A Historical Study*. Nashville: Abingdon, 1960.

*D. Martin Luthers Werke*. [WA] Kritische Gesamtausgabe. 73 vols. Weimar: Nachfolger, 1883-2009.

Ebeling, Gerhard. "Karl Barths Ringen mit Luther." In *Lutherstudien* 3:428-574. Tübingen: Mohr/Siebeck, 1985.

———. "The Significance of the Critical Historical Method for Church and Theology in Protestantism." In *Word and Faith*, 17-61. Translated by J. W. Leitch. Philadelphia: Fortress, 1964.

Eckhardt, Burnell F., Jr. *Anselm and Luther on the Atonement: Was It 'Necessary'?* San Francisco: Mellen Research University Press, 1992.

Edwards, Mark U., Jr. *Luther's Last Battles: Politics and Polemics: 1531-46*. Ithaca: Cornell University Press, 1983.

Erb, Peter, trans. *Pietists: Selected Writings*. Classics of Western Spirituality. New York: Paulist, 1983.

Ericksen, Robert B. *Theologians under Hitler: Gerhard Kittel, Paul Althaus and Emanuel Hirsch*. New Haven: Yale University Press, 1985.

Flett, John G. *The Witness of God: The Trinity, Missio Dei, Karl Barth, and the Nature of Christian Community*. Grand Rapids: Eerdmans, 2010.

Forde, Gerhard O. *On Being a Theologian of the Cross: Reflections on Luther's Heidelberg Disputation, 1518*. Grand Rapids: Eerdmans, 1997.

Forell, George W., and James F. McCue, eds. *Confessing the One Faith: A Joint Commentary on the Augsburg Confession by Lutheran and Catholic Theologians*. Minneapolis: Augsburg, 1982.

Francke, August Hermann. "Autobiography." In *Pietists: Selected Writings*. Translated by Peter Erb. Classics of Western Spirituality. New York: Paulist, 1983.

Gerhard, Johannes. *Theological Commonplaces*. Translated by Richard J. Ginda. St. Louis: Concordia, 2009-.

Gerrish, B. A. *Grace and Reason: A Study in the Theology of Luther*. 1962. Reprint, Eugene, OR: Wipf & Stock, 2005.

## Bibliography

———. "The Reformation and the Rise of Modern Science." In *The Old Protestantism and the New: Essays on the Reformation Heritage*, 163–78. Chicago: University of Chicago Press, 1982.

Green, Lowell C. *Lutherans against Hitler: The Untold Story*. St. Louis: Concordia, 2007.

Gritsch, Eric W. *A History of Lutheranism*. Minneapolis: Fortress, 2002.

Gritsch, Eric W., and Robert W. Jenson. *Lutheranism: The Theological Movement and Its Confessional Writings*. Philadelphia: Fortress, 1978.

Haerle, Wilfried. "Rethinking Paul and Luther." *Lutheran Quarterly* 20 (2006) 303–17.

Haga, Joar. *Was There a Lutheran Metaphysics? The Interpretation of the* communicatio idiomatum *in Early Modern Lutheranism*. Refo500 Academic Studies 2. Göttingen: Vandenhoeck & Ruprecht, 2012.

Harrison, Verna. "Perichoresis in the Greek Fathers." *St. Vladimir's Theological Quarterly* 35 (1991) 53–65.

Heckel, Johannes. *Lex Charitatis: A Juristic Disquisition on Law in the Theology of Martin Luther*. Translated by Gottfried G. Krodel. Emory University Studies in Law and Religion. Grand Rapids: Eerdmans, 2010.

Hegel, G. F. W. *Lectures on the Philosophy of Religion*. The Lectures of 1827. Edited by Peter C. Hodgson. Berkeley: University of California Press, 1988.

Helmer, Christine. *How Luther Became the Reformer*. Louisville: Westminster John Knox, 2019.

———. *Theology and the End of Doctrine*. Louisville: Westminster John Knox, 2014.

———. *The Trinity and Martin Luther: A Study on the Relationship between Genre, Language and the Trinity in Luther's Works 1523–1546*. Veröffentlichungen des Instituts für Europäische Geschichte Mainz 174. Mainz: von Zabern, 1999.

Hendrix, Scott H. *Luther and the Papacy: Stages in a Reformation Conflict*. Philadelphia: Fortress, 1981.

———. *Recultivating the Vineyard: The Reformation Agendas of Christianization*. Louisville: Westminster John Knox, 2004.

Heschel, Susannah. *The Aryan Jesus: Christian Theologians and the Bible in Nazi Germany*. Princeton: Princeton University Press, 2008.

Hill, Wesley. *Paul and the Trinity: Persons, Relations, and the Pauline Letters*. Grand Rapids: Eerdmans, 2015.

## Bibliography

Hinlicky, Paul R. *Beloved Community: Critical Dogmatics after Christendom*. Grand Rapids: Eerdmans, 2015.

———. *Divine Simplicity: Christ the Crisis of Metaphysics*. Grand Rapids: Baker Academic, 2016.

———. "Irony of an Epithet: The Reversal of Luther's Enthusiasm in the Enlightenment." In *A Man of the Church: Honoring the Theology, Life, and Witness of Ralph Del Colle*, edited by Michel Barnes and Mickey L. Mattox, 302–15. Eugene, OR: Pickwick Publications, 2012.

———. *Luther and the Beloved Community: A Path for Christian Theology after Christendom*. Grand Rapids: Eerdmans, 2010.

———. *Luther for Evangelicals: A Reintroduction*. Grand Rapids: Baker Academic, 2017.

———. "Luther's Anti-Docetism in the *Disputatio de divinitate et humanitate Christi* (1540)." In *Creator est creatura: Luthers Christologie als Lehre von der Idiomenkommunikation*, edited by Oswald Bayer and Benjamin Gleede, 139–85. Theologische Bibliothek Töpelmann 138. Berlin: de Gruyter, 2007.

———. "Luther's Atheism." In *The Devil's Whore: Reason and Philosophy in the Lutheran Tradition*, edited by Jennifer Hockenbery Dragseth, 53–60. Studies in Lutheran History and Theology. Minneapolis: Fortress, 2011.

———. *Paths not Taken: Theology from Luther through Leibniz*. Grand Rapids: Eerdmans, 2009.

———. "The Reception of Luther in Pietism and the Enlightenment." In *The Oxford Handbook of Martin Luther's Theology*, edited by Robert Kolb et al., 540–50. Oxford Handbooks. Oxford: Oxford University Press, 2013.

———. "Verbum Externum: Dietrich Bonhoeffer's Bethel Confession." In *God Speaks to Us: Dietrich Bonhoeffer's Biblical Hermeneutics*, edited by Ralf K. Wüstenberg and Jens Zimmermann, 189–215. International Bonhoeffer Interpretations 5. Frankfurt: Lang: 2013.

Hitler, Adolf. *Mein Kampf*. Translated by Ralph Manheim. Boston: Houghton Mifflin, 1971.

Jenson, Robert W. *Systematic Theology*. 2 vols. New York: Oxford University Press, 1997.

———. *Unbaptized God: The Basic Flaw in Ecumenical Theology*. Minneapolis: Fortress, 1992.

Jüngel, Eberhard. *The Freedom of a Christian: Luther's Significance for Contemporary Theology*. Translated by Roy A. Harrisville. Minneapolis: Augsburg, 1988.

## Bibliography

———. *God as the Mystery of the World: On the Foundation of the Theology of the Crucified One in the Dispute between Theism and Atheism*. Translated by Darrell L. Guder. 1983. Reprint, Eugene, OR: Wipf & Stock, 2009.

———. *Justification: The Heart of the Christian Faith. A Theological Study with an Ecumenical Purpose*. Translated by Jeffrey F. Cayzer. Edinburgh: T. & T. Clark, 2001.

———. *Theological Essays I*. Edited by J. B. Webster. Edinburgh: T. & T. Clark, 1989.

Kant, Immanuel. *Critique of Judgment*. Translated by Werner S. Pluhar. Indianapolis: Hackett, 1987.

———. *Lectures on Philosophical Theology*. Translated by Allen W. Wood and Gertrude M. Clark. Ithaca, NY: Cornell University Press, 1978.

———. *Religion and Rational Theology*. Translated by Allen W. Wood and George Di Giovanni. Cambridge Edition of the Works of Immanuel Kant. Cambridge: Cambridge University Press, 1996.

Käsemann, Ernst. *New Testament Questions for Today*. Translated by W. J. Montague. Philadelphia: Fortress, 1979.

Kitamori, Kazoh. *Theology of the Pain of God*. 1965. Reprint, Eugene, OR: Wipf & Stock, 2005.

Kojeve, Alexandre. *Introduction to the Reading of Hegel: Lectures on the Phenomenology of Spirit*. Translated by James H. Nichols Jr. Ithaca, NY: Cornell University Press, 1996.

Kolb, Robert. *Bound Choice, Election, and Wittenberg Theological Method: From Martin Luther to the Formula of Concord*. Lutheran Quarterly Books. Grand Rapids: Eerdmans, 2005.

Kolb, Robert, and Timothy J. Wengert, eds. *The Book of Concord: The Confessions of the Evangelical Lutheran Church*. Minneapolis: Fortress, 2000.

Kuehn, Manfred. "The Inaugural Dissertation: 'Genuine Metaphysics without Any Admixture of the Sensible.'" In *Kant: A Biography*, 188–93. Cambridge: Cambridge University Press, 2001.

LaVopa, Anthony J. "The Philosopher and the *Schwärmer*: On the Career of a German Epithet from Luther to Kant." *Huntington Library Quarterly* 60 (1997) 85–115.

Lienhard, Marc. *Martin Luther: Witness to Jesus Christ, Stages and Themes of the Reformer's Christology*. Translated by Edwin H. Robertson. Minneapolis: Augsburg, 1982.

Lilla, Mark. *The Stillborn God: Religion, Politics, and the Modern West*. New York: Knopf, 2007.

## Bibliography

Lohse, Bernard. *Martin Luther's Theology: Its Historical and Systematic Development.* Translated by Roy A. Harrisville. Minneapolis: Fortress, 1999.

Lotz, David. *Ritschl and Luther: A Fresh Perspective on Albrecht Ritschl's Theology in the Light of His Luther Study.* Nashville: Abingdon, 1974.

Lund, Eric, ed. *Documents from the History of Lutheranism, 1517–1750.* Minneapolis: Fortress, 2002.

Luther, Martin. *The Bondage of the Will.* Translated by J. I. Packer and O. R. Johnston. Grand Rapids: Revell, 1957, reprinted 2000.

Luther, Martin. *Luther's Works* [LW]. Edited by Jaroslav Pelikan, Helmut T. Lehmann, and Christopher Boyd Brown. 75 vols. Philadelphia: Muhlenberg and Fortress. St. Louis: Concordia, 1955–.

The Lutheran Church Missouri Synod. "A Statement of Scriptural and Confessional Principles." St. Louis: Concordia, 1973. https://www.lcms.org/about/beliefs/doctrine/statement-of-scriptural-and-confessional-principles.

Mannermaa, Tuomo. *Der im Glauben Gegenwaertige Christus: Rechtferigung und Vergottung zum oekumenischen Dialog.* Arbeiten zur Geschichte und Theologie des Luthertums, N.F. 8. Hannover: Lutherisches Verlagshaus, 1989.

Massing, Michael. *Fatal Discord: Erasmus, Luther and the Fight for the Western Mind.* New York: HarperCollins, 2017.

Mattes, Mark C. *The Role of Justification in Contemporary Theology.* Lutheran Quarterly Books. Grand Rapids: Eerdmans, 2004.

Mauer, Wilhelm. *Historical Commentary on the Augsburg Confession.* Translated by H. George Anderson. Philadelphia: Fortress, 1986.

Meyendorff, John. *Byzantine Theology: Historical Trends and Doctrinal Themes.* New York: Fordham University Press, 1979.

———. *Christ in Eastern Christian Thought.* Crestwood, NY: St. Vladimir's Seminary Press, 1987.

Meyer, Rudolf W. *Leibniz and the Seventeenth-Century Revolution.* Translated by J. P. Stern. Cambridge: Bowes & Bowes, 1952.

Oberman, Heiko A. *The Dawn of the Reformation: Essays in Late Medieval and Early Reformation Thought.* Edinburgh: T. & T. Clark, 1986.

———. *The Harvest of Medieval Theology: Gabriel Biel and Late Medieval Nominalism.* Grand Rapids: Baker Academic, 2000.

———. *Luther: Man between God and the Devil.* Translated by Eileen Walliser-Schwarzbart. New Haven: Yale University Press, 1989.

## Bibliography

———. *The Roots of Anti-Semitism in the Age of Renaissance and Reformation.* Translated by J. I. Porter. Philadelphia: Fortress, 1984.

O'Regan, Cyril. *The Heterodox Hegel.* SUNY Series in Hegelian Studies. Albany: SUNY Press, 1994.

Pannenberg, Wolfhart. *Systematic Theology.* Translated by Geoffrey W. Bromiley. 3 vols. Grand Rapids: Eerdmans, 1991–98.

Paulson, Steven D. *Lutheran Theology.* London: T. & T. Clark, 2011.

Pelikan, Jaroslav. *From Luther to Kirkegaard: A Study in the History of Theology.* St. Louis: Concordia, 1950.

———. *Obedient Rebels: Catholic Substance and Protestant Principle in Luther's Reformation.* New York: Harper & Row, 1964.

Peterson, Cheryl M. *Who Is the Church? An Ecclesiology for the 21st Century.* Minneapolis: Fortress, 2013.

Prenter, Regin. *Spiritus Creator.* Translated by John M. Jensen. Philadelphia: Muhlenberg, 1953.

Preus, Herman A., and Edmund Smits, eds. *The Doctrine of Man in Classical Lutheran Theology.* Minneapolis: Augsburg, 1962.

Preus, Robert D. *The Theology of Post-Reformation Lutheranism.* 2 vols. St. Louis: Concordia, 1972.

Raitt, Jill. *The Colloquy of Montbeliard: Religion and Politics in the Sixteenth Century.* Oxford: Oxford University Press, 1993.

Ritschl, Albrecht. *The Christian Doctrine of Justification and Reconciliation: The Positive Development of the Doctrine.* Translated by H. R. MacIntosh and A. B. McCaulay. Clifton, NJ: Reference Books, 1966.

———. *Three Essays: Theology and Metaphysics, Prolegomena to the History of Pietism, Instruction in the Christian Religion.* Translated by Philip Hefner. 1972. Reprint, Eugene, OR: Wipf & Stock, 2005.

Saarinen, Risto. *Gottes Wirken auf Uns: Die transzendentale Deut-ung des Gegenwart-Christi-Motivs in der Lutherforschung.* Veröffentlichungen des Instituts für Europäische Geschichte Mainz 137. Stuttgart: Steiner, 1989.

Schlink, Edmund. *The Doctrine of Baptism.* Translated by Herbert J. A. Bouman. St. Louis: Concordia, 1972.

Schmid, Heinrich. *The Doctrinal Theology of the Evangelical Lutheran Church.* 3rd ed. Philadelphia: Lutheran Publication Society, 1899.

Schmidt, Martin. "Spener und Luther: Noch zum 250. Todestag Philipp Jakob Speners am 5. Februar 1955." *Luther-Jahrbuch* 26 (1957) 102–29. Berlin: Lutherisches Verlagshaus, 1957.

# Bibliography

Schroeder, H. J., OP, trans. *Canons and Decrees of the Council of Trent.* St. Louis: Herder, 1960.

Schulze, Manfred. "Martin Luther and the Church Fathers." In *The Reception of the Church Fathers in the West: From the Carolingians to the Maurists*, edited by Irene Backus, 573–626. Leiden: Brill, 1997.

Skinner, Quentin. *The Foundations of Modern Political Thought.* Vol. 2, *The Age of Reformation.* Cambridge: Cambridge University Press, 1978.

Smith, Leonard S. *Religion and the Rise of History: Martin Luther and the Cultural Revolution in Germany, 1760–1810.* Eugene, OR: Cascade Books, 2009.

Soskice, Janet. *Metaphor and Religious Language.* Oxford: Clarendon, 1987.

Spener, Philip Jacob. *Pia Desideria.* Translated by Theodore G. Tappert. Seminar Editions. Philadelphia: Fortress, 1964.

Spinoza, Baruch. *Principles of Cartesian Philosophy* with *Metaphysical Thoughts.* Translated by Samuel Shirley. Indianapolis: Hackett, 1998.

Steves, Rick, dir. *Luther and the Reformation, 2017.* DVD.

Steigmann-Gall, Richard. *The Holy Reich: Nazi Conceptions of Christianity, 1919–1945.* Cambridge: Cambridge University Press, 2003.

Stoeffler, F. Ernst. *German Pietism during the Eighteenth Century.* Studies in the History of Religions 24. Leiden: Brill, 1973.

———. *The Rise of Evangelical Pietism.* Studies in the History of Religions 9. Leiden: Brill, 1965.

Troeltsch, Ernst. "Leibniz und die Anfänge des Pietismus." In *Gesammelte Schriften.* 4 vols. Tübingen: Mohr/Siebeck, 1912–25.

Vainio, Olli-Pekka. *Justification and Participation in Christ: The Development of the Lutheran Doctrine of Justification from Luther to the Formula of Concord (1580).* Studies in Medieval and Reformation Traditions 130. Leiden: Brill, 2008.

Witte, John, Jr. *Law and Protestantism: The Legal Teachings of the Lutheran Reformation.* Cambridge: Cambridge University Press, 2002.

# INDEX OF NAMES

Adam, 16, 39–41, 59
Althaus, Paul, 108–9, 113
Amos, 102
Aquinas, Thomas, 15
Aristotle, 9–10, 15, 59, 91
Arius, 29, 73
Arndt, Johann, 76–78
Athanasius, 29, 164
Augustine, 15–16, 40, 60, 122, 140
Ayres, Lewis, 144

Barth, Karl, xi, 6–7, 79, 103, 106, 108–9, 111–17, 119–21, 130–31, 141–42, 166
Baur, Ferdinand Christian, 105
Bayer, Oswald, 110, 154, 157–60
Bergen, Doris, 119
Bernard, 77
Bertram, Robert W, 158

Bethge, Eberhard, 109
Biel, Gabriel, 15
Bielfeldt, Dennis, 141
Bismarck, Otto, 111
Boehme, Jakob, 145
Bonhoeffer, Dietrich, 20, 47, 102, 109–11, 113, 116, 126–32, 133, 135, 139–40
Boye, Birgitte, xiii
Braaten, Carl, 157, 160–61
Brecht, Martin, 81–83
Brenz, Johannes, 69, 72
Brown, Dale, 80
Brunner, Emil, 113
Bultmann, Rudolf, 45–46, 106, 109–11, 115, 117–24, 152
Busch, Eberhard, 79

Calvin, John, 54
Cassirer, Ernst, 89

## Index of Names

Cicero, 44
Columbus, Christopher, 91
Constantine, 10, 53
Copernicus, Nicolaus, 91
Cyril of Alexander, 67

Dalferth, Ingolf U., 152
Darwin, Charles, 91
David, 17, 47, 98
DeJonge, Michael, 109
Dillenberger, John, 91
Dorner, Isaiah, 104

Eck, Johannes, 82
Elert, Werner, 108–9, 113
Erasmus, 1, 9, 37–40, 42–45, 56–57
Erb, Peter, 76, 81
Ericksen, Robert, 87

Fedde, Elisabeth, xiii
Feuerbach, Ludwig, xi, 103
Fichte, Immanuel, 94
Flacius, Mathias, 59
Flett, John, 115
Forde, Gerhard, 117
Forell, George, 37
Francke, August Hermann, 80–81

Gerhard, Johann, 64, 67, 70–73
Gleede, Benjamin, 154
Green, Lowell, 113
Gritsch, Eric, 76–77

Hamann, Johann Georg, 110, 160
Harnack, Adolf, 88, 105, 112, 132–33
Harnack, Theodosius, 105
Harrison, Verna, 143

Hegel, Georg Wilhelm Friedrich, 12, 69–70, 104–5, 111–12, 118, 143–46, 150–52
Helmer, Christine, 5, 85, 88
Henry VIII, 52
Hill, Wesley, 72
Hinlicky, Paul, 42, 66–67, 74, 86, 129, 140, 142, 146
Hitler, Adolf, 20, 87–88, 95, 108–9, 111, 113, 135, 152
Holl, Karl, 88, 112

Jenson, Robert W, xi, 56, 104, 110, 139, 142, 146–51, 158–60, 162
Jesus, xii, 6, 11, 13, 17–21, 28–34, 37, 39, 45–46, 48–49, 57, 61, 65–70, 73, 84–85, 90, 101, 104, 114–15, 117–18, 120–21, 123, 125–30, 137, 139, 141, 147, 153, 155, 159–61, 169
John of Damascus, 68
Joshua, 17, 47

Kant, Immanuel, 6, 11, 44, 74, 86, 92–99, 104–5, 110, 128, 168
Karlstadt, Andreas, 31, 82, 126–28
Käsemann, Ernst, 122–23
Kierkegaard, Søren, 6–7, 107, 118, 160
Kitamori, Kazoh, 102, 110, 157, 161–65, 167
Kojève, Alexandre, 144
Kolb, Robert, 5, 50, 57

## Index of Names

Leo, Pope 30
Lilla, Mark, 42
Lotz, David, 102

Mannermaa, Tuomo, 75
Marcion, 132
Marx, Karl, 87
Mary, 30, 67, 104
Massing, Michael, 1
Mattes, Mark, 158
Maurer, Wilhelm, 141
McCue, James F., 37
Melanchthon, Philip, 9, 53–55, 58, 60–62, 66
Meyendorff, John, 70–71
Meyer, R., 80–81
Moltmann, Jürgen, 48, 158
Morimoto, Anri, 163
Moses, 47

Nietzsche, Friedrich, 87, 96, 107, 151–52

O'Regan, Cyril, 144
Oberman, Heiko, 75–77, 79
Occam, William, 15, 57
Osiander, Andreas, 60–63, 124

Paul the Apostle, 16–17, 21–22, 24, 44, 49, 53, 62, 64, 72, 102, 112, 114–15, 117, 119, 122–23, 154
Peterson, Cheryl, 161
Pilate, Pontius, 45, 67, 104
Plato, 85
Preus, Jacob, 63
Preus, Ralph, 64

Raitt, Jill, 58
Ritschl, Albrecht, 10–11, 74–76, 79, 98–100, 102
Saarinen, Risto, 75

Sandell, Lina, xiii
Sasse, Hermann, 20, 109, 129–30, 133
Schelling, Friedrich, 124
Schmid, Heinrich, 63
Schmidt, Martin, 77
Scotus, Duns, 15
Shirer, William L., 111
Skinner, Quentin, 52
Soskice, Janet, 90–91
Spener, Philipp Jakob, 76–78, 80
Spinoza, Baruch, 89, 103
Stalin, Joseph, 152
Steigmann-Gall, Richard, 119
Steves, Rick, 1
Stoeffler, F. Ernst, 78
Storch, Nicolas, 82

Tauler, Johannes, 76–77, 81–82
Tertullian, 156
Tillich, Hannah, 123
Tillich, Paul, 35, 106–7, 109, 111, 123–25
Tumsa, Gudina, xii

Vainio, Olli-Pekka, 58
Vind, Anna, 154
von Grumbach, Argula, xiii
von Greiffenberg, Catterina Regina, xiii

Wengert, Timothy, 5, 50
Wilson, Sarah Hinlicky, xi, 167
Witte, John Jr., 50
Wolterstorff, Nicholas, 148
Wrede, Mathilda

Ziegenbalg, Bartholomäus, xii
Žižek, Slavoj, 70, 144, 146
Zwingli, Huldrych, 31, 41, 54, 64

CPSIA information can be obtained
at www.ICGtesting.com
Printed in the USA
LVHW041731260423
745301LV00004B/208

9 781498 234092